RENEW YOURSELF

RENEW
YOURSELF

A Six-Step Plan *for* More
Meaningful Work

CATHERINE HAKALA-AUSPERK

AN IMPRINT OF THE AMERICAN LIBRARY ASSOCIATION

CHICAGO   2017

Catherine Hakala-Ausperk is a 31-year public library veteran with experience in everything from customer service to management and administration. Now an active library planner, speaker, consultant, and trainer, she is also the author of *Be a Great Boss: One Year to Success* (2011) and *Build a Great Team: One Year to Success* (2013). Hakala-Ausperk is an adjunct faculty member at Kent (Ohio) State University's School of Library and Information Science, and she also teaches for the American Library Association's Certified Public Library Administrator (CPLA) Program, as well as for InfoPeople. Nationally, she keynotes, presents, and facilitates workshops, seminars, leadership academies, and staff days. Hakala-Ausperk's blog is published by Demco and is entitled *Library Advice: That's a Great Question!* She is also the editor of "By the Book," a professional book review column in *Public Libraries* magazine. She is the owner of Libraries Thrive Consulting (librariesthrive.com). Hakala-Ausperk's passion is for supporting, coaching, and developing great libraries with successful team members, and—especially—strong and effective library leaders.

© 2017 by the American Library Association

Extensive effort has gone into ensuring the reliability of the information in this book; however, the publisher makes no warranty, express or implied, with respect to the material contained herein.

ISBNs
978-0-8389-1499-1 (paper)
978-0-8389-1518-9 (PDF)
978-0-8389-1519-6 (ePub)
978-0-8389-1520-2 (Kindle)

Library of Congress Cataloging-in-Publication Data
Names: Hakala-Ausperk, Catherine.
Title: Renew yourself : a six-step plan for more meaningful work / Catherine
    Hakala-Ausperk.
Description: Chicago : ALA Editions, an imprint of the American Library
    Association, 2017. | Includes bibliographical references.
Identifiers: LCCN 2016034630| ISBN 9780838914991 (pbk. : alk. paper) | ISBN
    9780838915189 (pdf) | ISBN 9780838915196 (epub) | ISBN 9780838915202
    (kindle)
Subjects: LCSH: Vocational guidance. | Vocational guidance—Problems,
    exercises, etc. | Job satisfaction. | Self-realization.
Classification: LCC HF5381 .H35 2016 | DDC 650.1—dc23 LC record available at
    https://lccn.loc.gov/2016034630

Cover design by Alejandra Diaz. Images © Shutterstock, Inc.
Book design and composition in the Minion Pro and Brandon Grotesque typefaces
by Ryan Scheife, Mayfly Design.

♾ This paper meets the requirements of ANSI/NISO Z39.48–1992 (Permanence of Paper).

Printed in the United States of America

21 20 19 18 17   5 4 3 2 1

With immeasurable gratitude to my best friend,
who also happens to be my husband, for his never-ending support.

CONTENTS

Why Bother? 71

How Do You Do It? 87

A PDF of "My Renewal Plan" is available for download on the author's website, http://librariesthrive.com/New/renew-six -step-plan-meaningful-work/.

(LIBRARIAN TO A CUSTOMER WHO IS RETURNING A BOOK ON LIFE):

"Are you finished with this? Are you returning it?"

(CUSTOMER'S RESPONSE):

"No, I'm not finished. I'm going to renew it.
I'd like to get more out of it this time around."

PREFACE

Why Did I Write This Book?

This book is not about how to quit your job and go live on the beach and sell souvenir seashells. It's about meeting a much more real and pressing need to not *just work,* but to be happier and more fulfilled while doing it.

I'm lucky. In my work, I am privileged to have the chance to travel around the country, helping new leaders build skills, helping teams strengthen, and helping organizations plan. Lots of times, all of this seems to begin to look like therapy. Why? Because the challenges I encounter and the stories I hear can rarely be solved by fixing the organization—but more often by strengthening *and renewing* the people who work in them.

No matter what their age, lots of people don't seem to really know what they want to be when they grow up. They're still searching, not to figure out what they love to do, but how to make it a part of their working life.

This book is for all those people I've known in my thirty-plus years spent working in libraries who have confided in me that, whether they're happy in their current job or they hate it, something *else* just seems to be missing. There's something inside them that they really, really want to do—to accomplish or to contribute, but they just don't know for sure what it is and they certainly don't have any idea how to go about finding out.

Hopefully, this book and its six-step process will help to resolve that problem.

This book isn't meant to be therapy. It's meant to be fun . . . and meaningful.

Why Are You Reading It?

All the people I'm talking about have something in common—and you probably do too. They're filled with passion, skills, experience and drive—they're just lacking direction.

We all know that this isn't a dress rehearsal. We're on the clock . . . all of us . . . which is likely why you are reading this book in the first place. Have you ever said, "*I just don't know what I really want to do!*"? If so, I hope this book will help you to figure that out. You might find the answer by adding something special to what you do now. Or you may end up realizing you need a more significant change. Maybe, it's just a new department or title that you need—or perhaps it's something more significant than that.

The point is to really stop, read, and think about what you love the most and how you can use that to energize and *renew* yourself and your future. This book is a pathway to help you do just that. Or maybe you only want to figure out, once and for all, how to spend your time, talents, and energy. This book will help you do that, too.

What this book will *not* do is provide all the answers for you. You will do that yourself, by completing the reflections and exercises and developing your own, unique *Renewal Plan*. (The plan is in the back of this book, so you can go ahead and take a look at it, but don't be tempted to jump to filling it in on your own. Let this process do its work and help you spend the time you need to figure out just who you really are.)

If someone told you that by reading just a few pages and completing a six-step plan, you could find a way to feel more useful, more engaged, and just plain happier about getting up every morning, would you do it? I hope so. I can guarantee only one thing . . . you're worth it. We all are.

INTRODUCTION

How Does This Book Work?

One of the first things writers learn is to *keep it simple*.

Start with the basics, then build to the bigger picture. Reporters begin, then, by providing the *who, what, when, where, why, and how* of what they're trying to describe. If that's done well, the reader then becomes part of the story.

This book poses those questions and hopefully, as each reader does the work necessary to fill in the answers, even something as complex as finding more meaning in your life can be seen clearly.

Once our path is clear, we can achieve.

5W1H

There are a lot of complicated ways to consider how to move through life and work.

This isn't one of them.

Since you are the one who picked up this book, it's fair to say you just want to take another shot, not just at going through the motions every day, but at actually accomplishing something that matters.

Contrary to what most people grow up thinking, work and life are not mutually exclusive. Finding meaning in one—or the lack thereof—is going to impact the other. The good news is, at absolutely any point in your life, you can rewind and restart.

You can renew.

A great retirement greeting card reads "*Some people don't just make a career; they make a difference.*" That's what this book is going to help you do . . . and here's how. Let's talk a little bit more about 5W1H. As all young journalism students learn first, getting the answers to *who, what, when, where, why, and how* is the basic recipe for understanding any story. And your career, after all, is your story.

Put simply, "the five Ws and one H are questions whose answers are considered basic in information-gathering or problem-solving."[1] That's why they are the very first thing new reporters learn, because they are the best formula for "getting the complete story."[2] If they're good enough not only for the press, but for Cicero, Thomas Aquinas, and Rudyard Kipling,[3] then they should work for our process today. This book will delve into each of these steps more closely in the coming pages. What's important now is understanding what they can help you to do.

Do you want to (or do you have to) stay right where you are? Then this simple reexamination of your life might just help you to blend a way to both pay the bills and have an impact doing something you love. Maybe you are choosing a career, deciding on a college, or picking a retirement date. No matter what the timing or direction, considering and identifying *your* story could make any of those decisions come out right not just for *you* but for your *purpose.*

As already promised, what will result from considering your story and completing the exercises in this book is your own personal *Renewal Plan,* which will provide you with both the incentive and the pathway to positive change.

Facebook has arguably become the new Burma Shave sign of our times and, recently, a particularly poignant thought—applicable to this journey—was shared. It read: *I expected getting old to take longer.*

But, in actuality, it doesn't. So, to do it right the first time, to do it in a way we can appreciate, enjoy, and be proud of, we need a map. Or a plan. Or a mapped-out plan that we can update periodically when life hands us a turn before the road actually curves. The plan you're about to create isn't just a fill-in-the-blank or multiple-choice assignment. I'll prompt you in each section, helping you to develop your thoughts into action. One warning . . . be sure to not jump ahead. With each chapter you complete, you'll be thoughtfully considering some critical questions, all of which will point you towards your own success.

Sounds pretty simple, right? So do you really need to read a book to fill this out? Maybe not. But, in the process of filling in all these blanks, you're going to finally give yourself the time to really think about you, your values, your dreams, your goals, your realities, and your future. By working through each section in this book, you'll be developing an updated, focused, important revelation about how you want to matter.

The best part is, you may not even need to go anywhere or do anything differently to succeed in this plan. You don't have to quit your job. (Although you might end up taking a new job. Maybe.) You don't have to get another degree, develop an award-winning resume, or schmooze with movers and shakers (although any of those things *might* happen). You don't need a big new title or a corner office (although those might come along too, some day).

This is just a simple process to encourage you (and allow you) time to think, to consider, and then to act. Intentionally.

This book is about and for you. Period. Even if you're feeling stuck in a dead-end job with *no* chance to move on, you still have roughly sixteen *other* hours in your day that *you* control. You can fill those hours any way you want and still have time for the eight that pay the bills. Or, who knows, once you get the hang of this annual renewal, you can probably combine the two.

Some of the points in this book will be told as stories, and there is something you need to know about them. They're true. You might even see yourself in some of them...

There was a woman in what many might consider a dead-end clerical job. With limited education, there wasn't anywhere else for her to go in that particular organization, so she could easily have become disillusioned, cynical, and even angry about her boring day-to-day tasks. (Sound like anyone you know?) But she was dedicated to lifting others up and so she became the in-house mentor for every new clerical hire. Unofficially, of course.

On her own time, she read about and developed mentoring and coaching skills far beyond what her current job description would have allowed. Unofficially, she took one new staffer after another under her wing and made sure they felt and were successful. They moved on, many of them, but they never forgot her kindness and support. And she never forgot how her engagement with them enhanced her day-to-day work. Although she is still in the same "paying" position today and is still doing the same tasks, she is renewed because she committed to making that difference. In her little spot of the world, she mattered.

We all can.

So, how will this book help you to write your Renewal Plan? The answer is by keeping it simple—and going back to 5W1H, which go like this...

WHO
WHAT
WHEN
WHERE
WHY
HOW

Once more, please, don't try to jump to the end of the book to fill out that plan. It'll be fun and rewarding to take your own life tour and come up with your own realities. Write in this book! Or, if you've borrowed it from a library, pick up a notebook you can use as you move along.

In the end, you may be focused on an entirely new project that sends you in a brand new direction, or else you'll know that your everyday actions are right on target. But, either way, that target—and you—will be renewed.

So, let's get to work on the first part of 5W1H . . . Who are you, really?

NOTES

1. *Wikipedia*, s.v., "Five Ws," https://en.wikipedia.org/wiki/Five_Ws.
2. Ibid.
3. "7 Key Questions: Who, What, Why, When, Where, How, How Much?—Consultant's Mind," Consultant's Mind, July 24, 2015, www.consultantsmind.com/2015/07/24/7-key-questions/.

WHO ARE YOU?

When you know yourself, you are empowered.

When you accept yourself,

You are invincible.

—Tina Lifford

She ducked into the elevator just in time to miss some latecomers walking into her party. Not that she didn't appreciate the attention; she knew they meant well. "Congratulations on ten years in Technical Services," the banner in the staff room read! And it had been a good ten years, at least in part. Anna was happy in her work and she was good at it.

But, as the doors closed and she was alone with her thoughts, she realized that the problem was that there was something missing. Day in, day out, this just wasn't who she was. She wished there was some other way to both pay the bills and . . . to matter.

Right now, there was work piling up on her desk. She'd tackle that first, then she'd start thinking about a way to find . . . more. If there was one thing she knew for sure, it's that the next ten years—and the ones after that—were going to fly by, too.

Introductions

The process you're going to experience throughout this book needs to start by looking backwards.

Are you just starting out on your career path and, with so many (or maybe so few) options to choose from, you're just not sure which way to go? Or perhaps you're feeling a little burned out (plateauing, as the experts call it) and you're thinking it's time for a change? Maybe you don't want too much of a change but would prefer to stay where you are ... and be just a little happier? Or perhaps you're at that new re-tirement stage that doesn't look anything like retirement used to look. You want to keep doing something, you think, but what?

Most everyone finds themselves in one of those spots at one time or another and that's why, lucky for us, there's a lot of good advice, mentoring, coaching, and information to help us move forward at ev-ery stage. So, what's the problem? The answers, no matter how well described, are never that easy to find. Most people do what they feel they're supposed to do when they think they're supposed to do it, and they put their personal ambitions aside for the common good. We can get to our dreams later, right?

Not always. The playing field is so very different today and the options are much wider. It's not that more options aren't there. It's just that most of us don't know how or don't take the time to look for them.

One thing's for sure, the traditional career ladder is gone. In its place in today's working world is a rock wall. I'm sure you can pic-ture it and maybe you've even experienced traveling around it on your personal journey. You go forward a little and then up. Backwards and sideways and then down. Over and around and, pretty soon, you're at a staff room anniversary party that's for you, and you're not really sure how you got there ... or why you stayed. The good news is, today's the day you can start making another move on the wall and this one can be for the right reasons.

A couple of points to get out of the way early on. This book is not a resume guide. This is not a list of job search tips or interview questions. As a matter of fact, this isn't really just a book at all—it's a project. And, as you work through it, it will put *you* more firmly, confidently, and intentionally in charge of your own future. Imagine a future that results in a *deliberate* career, one that mirrors your values, supports the life you want to live, and results in a contribution that matters to you.

Doesn't that sound better than *just* going to work?

But be forewarned: this book isn't meant to be just another quick read.

Renewal, as defined by Merriam-Webster, is "the state of being made new, fresh, or strong again."[1] In short, it's a verb. You are going to work on *renewing yourself,* starting here and now. To get the most out of this book, please don't skip over the assignments embedded in each section. By actually completing them, you'll be doing yourself a favor. You'll be finding an entirely new reason to get up every day and enjoy doing what you do.

You'll be making a living *and* making a difference.

So, let's start with that look back at how you got where you are today.

This book is predicated on the fact that, once you spend some time considering (or reconsidering, "renewing") what really matters to you, you can match it to how you want to spend the rest of your life and, therefore, pay the bills *and* find real joy.

If it's that simple, you might be wondering, why doesn't everyone do it? Well, many do. Executives leave high-paying, prestigious jobs to open food co-ops, and live happily ever after. Computer programmers turn into park rangers and accountants open day care centers for challenged kids. Take a look at this one—among many—examples. Roz Savage writes:

Why would a woman in her mid-30s, with no previous record of either adventure or insanity, quit her job, leave her husband and home, and set out to row around the world? No doubt many of my friends, and most certainly my mother, asked themselves this in 2004 when I announced my intention to row across the Atlantic Ocean.

I went on to row across the Pacific from 2008 to 2010 and the Indian Ocean last year, being the first woman to row across each of the three oceans. During my time on the water, the reason for my decision became increasingly clear—I had suffered a double-whammy of revelations that simply made my previous life direction untenable.

First, I realized that my job, although it paid me well, was not making me happy. One day, I sat down and wrote two versions of my own obituary: the one I wanted to have, and the one I was heading for if I carried on my current path. My job was not taking me the way that I wanted to go. It was, in fact, taking me in the opposite direction, toward a life of tedium and obligation rather than one of freedom and fulfillment.[2]

So, who are *you*?

Things That Really Matter

"What are you going to major in?"

Ever been asked that? Or maybe you've heard the dreaded interview question, "Where do you see yourself in five years?" Or, even worse yet, "Tell me about yourself."

These questions sound a lot easier than they are when we try to answer them succinctly. Who among us can say exactly what we hope to do—or even what we believe we're capable of—when we first start out in life? And, as a result, our careers ride the waves of the current or the economy or family dynamics, rather than follow a track of our own choosing that can provide us with personal reward or achievement.

It doesn't have to be that way. If we pause first (as you are doing right now) to think about who you really are and who you want to become, we can get back on our own road.

Great managers try hard to figure out what that road is when they're interviewing and making those critical decisions about whom to hire. Organizations that care not only about the knowledge and skills they're seeking but about the people will do so by trying to understand how the applicant sees herself. They might ask, "Tell us three words that describe you." This is what is sometimes called a *so what* question, not because self-realization isn't important, but because those three words are too easy to come up with and are rarely very telling. They often hear:

> *I'm honest, hard-working, and creative.*
> *I'm focused, experienced, and flexible.*
> *I'm dependable, trustworthy, and experienced.*

But what those answers might actually be saying (without really meaning to) is:

> *I'm practiced at interviewing, vague, and willing to try anything for a job.*

It's not our fault. As busy people caught up in a demanding world, the reality is we don't really know or often give much thought to who we are or what we want. For that reason, a much better interview question is, "Tell us *twenty* words that describe you." At this level of depth, a lot more can be learned. Try it.

But wait. First, there's one more interview tactic to apply here. When looking for a librarian with excellent readers' advisory skills, managers will often qualify their questions, so as to eliminate the *easy* ones. They might ask, for example, "Other than Nora Roberts, Patricia Cornwell, or Janet Evanovich, name five other popular fiction writers." A question like this will give amateur librarians pause (Geez, those are the easy ones I would have said!) and will help experienced readers stand out with their extensive knowledge of books and writers. Twenty instead of three. Now that's some deeper thinking.

Try it. Other than being hard-working, honest, and dependable, what twenty words best describe *you?*

Author Shana Montesol Johnson has a bit more advice for anyone attempting to explore their values. She describes them first as "the interests and qualities that you've always found yourself drawn to."[3] Trying not to think of our personal values in the same way that word is used in a general sense, she suggests some questions or measures we can use to determine what our values really are. Ask:

- Do you want it, but it doesn't come easily? (Then it's probably a "should," not a value.)
- Are you doing it in order to get something else? (If yes, not a value.)
- Did you do it when you were seven years old? (If yes, probably a value.)
- Is it really exciting and you're a bit afraid of it? (If yes, probably a value. Keep it.)[4]

Think now about who you are and what you value. Try answering this question, with this qualification. List twenty answers here (and don't stop until you've written them all) that could complete this sentence:

I want my life and my work to be centered around things I truly value. Other than family, friends, and good health, my top twenty values are:

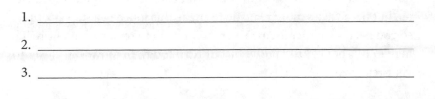

1. _____

2. _____

3. _____

4. _____

5. _____

6. _____

7. _____

8. _____

9. _____

10. _____

11. _____

12. _____

13. _____

14. _____

15. _____

16. _____

17. _____

18. _____

19. _____

20. _____

Here's the point of this exercise and, overall, of starting this renewal journey by finding out who we are. "Personal values are important because they provide us with a road map for the kind of life we aspire to lead. The more our choices line up with our values, the better we generally feel about ourselves."[5]

Now, reread your list. That's *who* you are. But you still have to get down to that magic number of three. Not because the others don't matter, but because it's more realistic to make this journey a step at a time, so you need a sharper focus. You're not trying to replan your entire life here in this book. Just take a twist or turn today, to move you closer to your real goals.

Let's borrow the creative way to do this that Roz Savage herself suggested. Have you ever considered writing your own obituary? That's what you're going to do next, at least the first part of it. Often used as part of a visioning process, doing this can actually help to sharpen your focus on values and separate what's real . . . from what we've been told should matter.

Remember, as an anonymous blogger once commented, "No one is going to stand up at your funeral and say 'She had a really expensive couch and great shoes.'"[6]

What would you prefer they say? Before you start writing, you need to narrow down your list a bit. Here's how to discover those top three values from your list. (This could take some time, but stick with it; the insight it will help you capture will be pivotal to the rest of your process.)

Reading through your list, put a #1 next to the value that means more to you than all the others. Rereading, put a #20 next to the one you could live without. (Remember, the sky's the limit in this exercise. Don't consider money or time or other realities; just go with what you truly feel.) Continue this process, making as many changes along the way as needed, until you've numbered them all.

Your Renewal Plan: Step One—Who?

Let's get started building your own, personal *Renewal Plan*. Complete the sentence below and then recopy your answers onto Lines #1, #2, and #3 in *Your Renewal Plan* in the back of this book.

The three things I most deeply value are:

1. _____

2. _____

3. _____

This is an important beginning. With those foundational values in place, further investigations both backward and forward are going to help design where you can go from here to make sure you are both honoring and implementing those values. Right now, it's time for that obituary. Just write the first paragraph or so that you would like to read, when the time comes. Make sure this paragraph somehow includes your most critical values.

(Your name here) was dedicated to _____

and made a significant contribution to _____

by her/his work in _____.

With the end in mind, let's go back to the beginning and then put this all together.

Life So Far . . .

Leaving the conceptual foundation of values alone for just a while, some practical reviewing of your life thus far will help continue the process of sharpening your focus.

Think back as far as you can and describe three things you've always wanted to do. Remember, these are things you *wanted to do*, not what you *wanted to be*. *(No one is reading this but you, so be honest! You can say cowgirl or astronaut if you want. As a matter of fact, that will be important later on.)*

1. _____

2. _____

3. _____

Do you see it? There should be a direct correlation between your newly identified values and what you've always wanted to *do*. Had you been accorded the opportunity to live in a perfect world, with plenty of time, money, and opportunity to chart your own course . . . ah, well. You're here now, and likely with a lot more intention and conviction than before. So, as a Roman philosopher once said, remember that "luck is what happens when preparation meets opportunity."[7] It's never too late to turn those values and dreams into reality.

In actuality, it's likely that you've already accomplished more than you realize or appreciate, albeit through channels other than what you expected. Take a look. What has your work life been like so far?

List the most recent ten jobs/positions you've held. If you haven't yet had that many, just list as many as you can remember. Leave the line underneath each job blank—for now.

1. _____

   _____

2. _____

   _____

3. _____

   _____

4. _____

   _____

5. _____

   _____

6. _____

   _____

7. _____

   _____

8. _____

   _____

9. _____

   _____

10. _____

   _____

Reviewing that list, on the line underneath each job you need to consider which of your twenty values you got to experience while there. In
order to do that, consider what really energized you at each position.
That's often how our values are *felt*. Ask yourself what work you found
most satisfying, which jobs fit your personality best, or what environment made you feel the most motivated.[8]

Obviously, since you've chosen to read this book, even though you
may have found partial matches to who you are and what you have
done, there are still gaps to be filled in. You can do that, here and now.

The Process

You've probably noticed by now that your life has taken some twists
and turns along the way. All for good reason, no doubt. Whatever you
feel at this point, don't be discouraged! To be honest, when we pause
like this to think back over where we've been, the whole idea of career
development has sort of a root canal feel to it. Even the words used to
describe *professional development* make it seem more challenging than
compelling.

We hear that we have to climb up ladders to be truly successful—
and that sounds dangerous. And some people don't just climb, we're
told, they *claw* their way to the top. Ouch. Then, once we get up there
(some of us in our *recommended* suits and heels), more than half of us
are taught to expect to crash into glass that we can't get through. The
rest of us are working our fingers to the bone. Having fun yet?

Don't believe it. Or at least, if that's all been true for you, you can
change that right now. If we take the time to look at our own career
path thus far, it really hasn't been all that terrible, has it? While we
didn't actually do anything wrong, we most likely followed our particular path hopefully, at best, and automatically, at worst. Not a bad start,
but we can do better for ourselves, our organizations, and our lives.

Since you've decided it's time to take a look forward, then there's
no better place to begin than by examining how you got to where you

are today. What you're likely to find are many intentional decisions that you're going to want to repeat. And with honest, open eyes, you'll probably also notice some Mulligans or choices you'd like to remake or, at the very least, not repeat. What this process can and should be is invigorating, uplifting, and encouraging—as far away from the root canal as we might have expected.

Remember, this is not (necessarily) an exercise that will lead you to a new job. That might not be at all what the new, renewed you discovers is the right move to make next. You might just end up realizing you are best off staying right where you are, but perhaps filling your day a little differently. Remember, "Growth isn't limited to movements over, up or down. With the right support, people can grow right where they're planted!"[9] Your goal should be to renew your commitment, your skills, your goals, and your future. Unfortunately, this isn't easy while we're busy working.

The woman we met in the introduction to this book, for example, probably stopped after realizing she could pay the bills and still get the kids on the bus on time. Worthy goals, both, but now that she's realized time won't wait for her to find more, she's going to go looking for a chance to matter. It's never too late.

You, too, have some clear ideas now and, hopefully, the enthusiasm to go with them to not only *look* ahead—but to *move* ahead with more purpose, clarity, and excitement. Why? Because those values you listed can help guide you to select, grow into, and develop a work life that matters—to you and to your employer—starting today. Everyone wins; organizations, those we impact, our families, and ourselves when reality finally gives way to intention.

That Old Life Ladder

Now that you've spent some time looking back, consider more carefully the personal career ladder you have happened to use. Did it work like this? "If you wanted to reach the upper rungs, unless you wanted to crawl on the backs of those ahead of you, you would have to wait your turn until the rung above you became available. And, if your ladder had rungs missing, you would have to take precarious, giant steps upward, not knowing for sure if you would safely make it to the next one up."[10]

While that may sound like the way we were told to expect professional fulfillment, it's not the only way, and certainly it's not the best—or the preferred! Still, if that's the path you've had to follow thus far . . . that's okay. Today is the first day of your *renewed* future. Let's examine some other options that will feel and work a whole lot better.

On our professional journey so far, most of us have tacked to cover,[11] as some less courageous sailors might do, by simply doing what others have done and what everyone expects of us. Authors Bennett and Miles explain that this might not be the best approach to take. "It's not always the best career strategy to follow the crowd. Sometimes, getting ahead requires the courage to break away from the pack."[12] And the same might be said for not *just* getting ahead and for being truly fulfilled in our work. Like captains in a sailboat race who don't tack but instead move courageously ahead, keeping to their own path, you might just find yourself "better off making career moves that head you in a different direction, where you can enjoy unique experience to . . . develop your talent and win in the future."[13]

Ok, Forget The Ladder!

Take a look around—and ahead—from where you are now. Regardless of *how* you got there, you've got a lot of turns yet to take, no matter where you are in your career. Forget the ladder. Once you've taken the time to clarify what you really want to do—and why—your options should look a lot more like that rock wall or, better yet, like a whitewashed, neighborly "lattice" (moving you) "across, up and down different positions"[14] until you feel focused, energized, and engaged in everything you do.

The next obvious question here is: why should you bother changing anything? Well, you made the lists when you answered the "values" questions. Consider now each and every day coming in your future—and how you want to reach and achieve them. Ask yourself, what's the best that can happen?

By matching what you rise to accomplish each day with your core values, you can actually be happy at work. Happy? Yes, the ultimate goal of your renewal will be happiness, which is what makes this entire exercise worthwhile. And, unlike pornography,[15] you don't have to *see* happiness to know you've discovered it. Gretchen Rubin, creator of "The Happiness Project," suggests you will have found yourself when what you do strengthens your relationship with other people. When your work provides you with novelty and challenge. When your path has not cost you too much loss in other areas of your life. When your work allows you to *Be (insert your name here)* instead of denying the truth of who you really are.[16]

We need to start by identifying our values, because "implementing them energizes everything."[17] It's time to get to work.

Try a New Focus

Experts tell us that the closer we get to our values, the more joy we feel. You may have felt it at first. Remember that very first day of that very first job that you really, really wanted? The trick, they tell us, is to find a place to work where that feeling lasts. Maybe there's even a bit of it left over for you now, but perhaps just not enough. Or maybe you feel that even though you've made the right moves on the lattice, right now you're just running out of gas.

The title of this section, "Try a New Focus," was chosen intentionally. It's meant to remind and entice you to consider what you still can do—to rechart your own course for the future. It's never too late! Read on.

In the coming chapters, you will continue to reexamine your current position in life—and in work, reconsider the footprint or contribution you want to make; recall and refocus on your dreams; refresh your reality; adjust your fit (which includes, of course, expanding your skills and options); recommit to tomorrow; reclaim your identity (not one thrust upon you by some dusty old job title); reinvent your brand, so as to sell yourself clearly; and, finally, celebrate your renewal.

You are moving forward, which is good, but you still don't know for sure when and where you'll arrive, which is even better. "Life is not a journey to the grave with the intention of arriving safely in a pretty and well preserved body, but rather to skid in broadside, thoroughly used up, totally worn out!"[18]

In the meantime, make sure you are keeping your reputation and your good name polished, so when you get there . . . someone or something will be waiting.

Stay Out of Your Way

Without even meaning to, and often without ever realizing it, we sometimes get in the way of our own future and trip over our own well-intentioned feet. Here are just a few suggestions, including some from Peter Economy, often called "The Leadership Guy," on how to avoid those pitfalls as your renewal continues. We'll think more about our day-to-day realities in future chapters, but throughout the entire process, we need to be sure that we're meeting our current commitments and responsibilities, even while planning our tomorrow.

- Don't burn bridges (you've heard this before, I'm sure). Just one unprofessional, disrespectful moment could ruin a career opportunity. Always treat others with respect and be professional—and stop the gossip chain—whether it is with your peers, the boss, clients, or customers. This applies to social media, too!

- Don't stop learning and challenging yourself. If you fall behind the times in knowledge and technology, and stubbornly continue down the old-trusted-ways road, your skills will eventually become out of date and completely obsolete. (*Author's note: I once met an employee, frustrated by a cut in her organization's training budget, who told me she was through with professional development. She even planned to let her professional certification lapse—if someone else wasn't going to pay for it anymore. That'll show 'em, huh?*)

- Don't let your resume gather dust. So often, when we land that great job, the resume is the first thing to bite the dust in the back of our desk. Don't build cobwebs—keep it handy and update it as new training, projects, and achievements come along (and do the same for your portfolio).

- Meet people. If you aren't networking and building a base of contacts, how do you expect anyone to know who you are?

- Give it your all. Every day. Or, as one of my favorite mentors always says . . . raise your hand! Show initiative at every opportunity and you'll find more of them coming your way.[19]

If it helps to embolden you on your renewal journey, realize you are not alone in this quest for a purposeful life. Consider these comments, collected over the years from anonymous employees who were probably feeling the same things you are thinking right now. Do you recognize yourself in one or more of them?

- Spending 40–60–80 hours somewhere each week . . . I want it to mean something. I want to feel like I'm moving forward somehow. If I can't grow here, I've gotta look elsewhere![20]

- Challenge me. Stretch me. I'm not as worried about being promoted as I am about learning, growing, and seeing my talents used in new and different ways![21]

- I'm happy at my current level. I don't ever want the headaches of being the boss. But I also don't want to stagnate where I am. I need to keep figuring out the next challenge, the next place I can make things happen.[22]

Misery Has Nothing to Do with It

Don't ignore this book just because you don't want people to think less of you for reading it. You don't have to hate your current job, or even feel hopeless in your current position in order to want to grow. Remember, as these years go by, we're talking about our *lives,* not just our *work* being spent. Renewal can rejuvenate you in any situation, whether you stay or leave your current position. Sometimes renewal can just unblock a dam of apathy, and with new energy can come new direction. I've never met a boss who wouldn't appreciate that in a staff member.

Maggie Zhang suggests several explanations for finding oneself in the quicksand of uncertainty and frustration at work:

1. Maybe you picked a conservative career when you were young and just never switched. Honestly, how many people really, really know what they want to do for thirty years when they just got out of high school?

2. You feel like you're working for the wrong reasons. One of the most common of those reasons? You feel like you're just following the money.

3. You feel like you're underused and just not working (as your grade school teacher used to say) up to your real potential.

4. You just can't find meaning in what you do. It goes against our basic human nature to do something for eight hours *just* to get money.

5. You don't feel in control. And you just never know what's going to happen next.

6. You work too much. You are overwhelmed and that concept of work-life balance you keep hearing about seems as likely as moving to Mars.[23]

Dr. Scott Sheperd warns "it is critical that we not miss our lives as we move through them."[24] I bet I can get an Amen for that!

So, are you ready to renew your life and career? By taking the time to refocus, you can reenergize. With time to rethink, you can redesign your imprint. Whether the concepts you'll consider in this book point you toward a different path altogether or help you gain momentum where you are right now, at least you'll know you are working for the right reasons.

It isn't just the work you do that deserves this type of effort. You do, too.

Two Final Exercises (these aren't part of your *Renewal Plan,* they are just to keep you moving forward to the next chapter. . .).

List three good reasons to finish this book.

1. _____

2. _____

3. _____

Finally, explain briefly why your career (and life) are worth renewing.

_____

_____

Whatever reason you just gave, I agree! Your renewal has begun! Next, we'll look at *what* those values should be directing you to do.

NOTES

1. "Simple Definition of Renewal," Merriam-Webster, http://1.www.merriam -webster.com/dictionary/renewal.
2. "9 Career Change Success Stories That Will Seriously Inspire You," The Muse, http://1.https://www.themuse.com/advice/why-i-quit-my-job-and -rowed-across-3-oceans.
3. Shana Montesol Johnson, "Do Not Make a Career Decision without This List," Development Crossroads, http://developmentcrossroads.com/2011/ 08/career-decision-list/.
4. Ibid.
5. "The Best Guide to Life: Your Personal Values," Wisconsin Relationship Education, http://wire.wisc.edu/yourself/selfreflectknowyourself/Your personalvalues.aspx.
6. "Quotes & Sayings," Enchanting Minds, "Quotes with Pictures," April 16, 2016, http://enchantingminds.net/no-one-is-going-to-stand-up-at-your -funeral-and-say-she-had-a-really-expensive-couch-and-great-shoes-dont -make-your-life-be-about-materialistic-stuff/.
7. "Popular Gambling and Betting Quotes and Sayings," Lootmeister.com, www .lootmeister.com/betting/quotes.php.

8. "Work Values—What Do You Find Really Important in Your Job?" 123Test, 2016, https://www.123test.com/work-values/.

9. Beverly Kaye and Julie Winkle Giulioni, *Help Them Grow or Watch Them Go: Career Conversations Employees Want* (San Francisco: Berrett-Koehler, 2012), 71.

10. Caitlin Williams and Annabelle Reitman, *Career Moves: Be Strategic about Your Future* (Alexandria, VA: American Society for Training and Development, 2013), 76.

11. Forum, Forbes Leadership, "How to Make Big Career Decisions: Don't Tack to Cover," *Forbes*, July 19, 2011, www.forbes.com/sites/forbesleader shipforum/2011/07/19/how-to-make-big-career-decisions-dont-tack-to -cover/#1373d95c5597.

12. Ibid.

13. Ibid.

14. Williams and Reitman, *Career Moves*, 76.

15. Peter Lattman, "The Origins of Justice Stewart's 'I Know It When I See It,'" *wsj.com*, September 28, 2007, http://blogs.wsj.com/law/2007/09/27/the -origins-of-justice-stewarts-i-know-it-when-i-see-it/.

16. Ken Wert, "7 Tips for Making Happy Decisions about How to Spend Your Time, Energy, and Money," Gretchen Rubin, "Efficiency," July 13, 2011, http://gretchenrubin.com/happiness_project/2011/07/7-tips-for-making -happy-decisions-about-how-to-spend-your-time-energy-and-money/.

17. Roy Posner, "A New Way of Living: Essays on Human Evolution and Transformation," Aurobindo.ru, 2010, http://1.http://www.aurobindo.ru/ workings/other/roy_posner-a_new_way_of_living.pdf.

18. "The 20 Greatest Hunter S. Thompson Quotes," Whizzpast, "Book Bash," October 7, 2013, www.whizzpast.com/20-greatest-hunter-s-thompson -quotes-voted-goodreads/.

19. "Want to Be Successful and Happy? Don't Make These 5 Deadly Career Mistakes," Inc.com, "Life," January 23, 2016, www.inc.com/peter-economy/ 5-career-mistakes-you-should-never-make.html.

20. Kaye and Giulioni, *Help Them Grow*, 7.

21. Ibid., 61.

22. Ibid., 62.

23. "Here's Why So Many People Hate Their Jobs," Business Insider, http://1 .http://www.businessinsider.com/reasons-you-hate-your-job-2014-6.

24. Harold J. Williams and Scott Sheperd, *Who's in Charge? Attacking the Stress Myth* (Highland City, FL: Rainbow Books, 1997), 50.

WHAT DO YOU WANT TO DO?

Great missions aren't about things that happen *to* you, they
are things that happen *through* you.

—Chad Delaney

*There weren't a lot of options when it came to where he was going to
work. It was a small town. To say that times were tough was an incredible understatement. Even with the rarity of a proffered scholarship, there
was no way his family could afford to cover the minimal balance, so his
future was sealed. For the next four decades, he sailed on huge ships that
carried everything from grain to iron ore from one end of the Great Lakes
to the other. Painting hulls, loading and unloading cargo, standing watch
and other mundane, repetitive, and often dangerous duties became his
life, and yet he was happy.*

*What did he do to achieve that happiness? He wrote poetry. He was
a writer deep down and he valued beauty and language. Years later, his
verses would be shared that described the industrial beauty of the glow
of frozen dew on dockside coal piles, or the ferocious, biting winds of
November gales. Animals, children, and of course the lake and life of a
mariner would be the beneficiaries of **what** he chose to do with the time
each day left to him that was his. What he did to survive was work. But
his mission was to use words to share beauty with others . . . so he wrote.*

The concept of mission revealed in the quote that opens this chapter
is a critical one. It represents probably the most precarious fork in the
road that we face when deciding where we want our career—and our
life—to go next. The wrong turn here can throw everything off the track.

The writer in the story, for example, could have described his mission as helping to move cargo over water . . . but one look at his values would tell you that work was a long way from the impact he truly

wanted to have. So his mission, even if he didn't pause to consider or accept it, was to write so that others could see beauty and love.

That's why the answer, if you're not thrilled with your current job, isn't *necessarily* to look for a new job. It just might be to find another way to share your values—and find your meaning.

Consider another example: a library that defines its mission as *to increase circulation.* Gathering that worthless statistic so as to heighten an arbitrarily perceived success is a mission *for* the library. Across the street, however, one might find an entirely different library, whose mission is to *enhance the lives of its residents.* Clearly, whatever actions move them toward success, whether those are a larger and more widely circulated collection or programs and classes on job searching and civic responsibility, will be achieved by their existence, actions, and passion that affect others.

Imagine the motivation to achieve, the sense of accomplishment and, put simply, the joy that comes from the latter, rather than the former's success.

It's the same with people. Consider an executive director who identifies his mission as *to amass wealth,* as opposed to a colleague who strives *to improve health conditions for all.* It would come as no surprise, then, that one of these people (the one looking for success to happen *for* him) will find less joy and fulfillment in his career than his counterpart, who looks to impact others. Maybe it's time for the first boss to renew . . . and redefine a mission that will matter. Then, what he could be saying is "Life has deep meaning to me now. I have discovered more than my ideal job; I have found my mission, and the reason why I am here on Earth."[1] A worthy goal, indeed, and the next step in your process of renewal.

Define Mission

If the word *mission* is starting to make this renewal concept sound suspiciously like a strategic plan to you, you're not too far from the truth, but please, don't let that put you off! Remember, this big-picture look at what you really hope to do is aimed at creating a future for yourself—at work and at home—that will matter. You started by thinking about who you really are and how you want to matter through your most significant values. Similarly, that's how strategy begins. And the next logical step is consideration of what you want to do about achieving that strategy—and that's your mission.

You can do that by looking first at what you've done, then at what you're doing now, and finally at what you *can* do—moving forward with a renewed commitment to your mission.

In the preceding chapter of this book, you defined what your most precious values are, and that was an important step in this process because "values are the core of every decision we make . . . You will find that your top 3–5 values are typically those for which you would fight. You will also likely find that they are among the things that you use to define yourself."[2]

Values are important to any decision-making process in your life because they represent your passion. If you'll fight for something, it must *really* matter! There's a direct correlation between that passion and the *what* part of what you should be doing. One author put this connection so succinctly as to call it a secret to your success. "Find what you are truly passionate about, and build your life's work around it."[3]

So your assignment here, in this chapter, is to discover what can happen when your passion and your values intersect. This will make your *mission* evident and will then suggest what you can do next in your career and in your life.

Put simply, this process is the opposite of not doing anything at all or, worse, continuing to spin on the same unfulfilling wheel that caused you to pick up this book in the first place. "If we don't ask what we can do or make or achieve or build, then we won't do or make or achieve or build. It's just that simple. Only through action is anything accomplished."[4]

What Is Work?

Missions matter, but they don't always come first, as they should. Even the most rudimentary review of why people get up in the morning, put both feet on the floor, and go to work must start with a recognition of life's basic needs. Back in the 1940s, a man named Abraham Maslow outlined them pretty clearly—and in a particular, logical order. Loosely translated, they look like this:

- First, we have to eat. And be hot or cold, as appropriate. So, food and shelter.
- Next, we need to be safe and healthy.
- Love (or some kind of human relationship) would be nice.
- Then, beyond that, respect would build our own confidence. (I guess we'd have to do something to earn that.)
- That's where mission comes in.[5]

For the purposes of your work in this chapter, we're going to assume that those first three needs (food, safety, and health) have been met, and now you're looking to achieve those final two levels of need by locating an opportunity to contribute, to feel fulfilled and—yes—to be happy. As leadership expert Meghan Biro says, "Happiness is a loaded word in our culture, and in our workplace cultures. It's important to keep in mind that we all have our own personal definition of happiness. But I firmly believe that a fulfilling career is a direct result of doing work that matters—that engages us [in] mind, heart and soul."[6]

Your True Identity

Most of us would answer the request "Describe yourself" with facts, figures, titles, and generalities. For example, I am a middle-aged former librarian with a husband, children, grandchildren, and friends, who loves to teach and write. Descriptions like these "have usually shaped our lives. They are experience, history, role, relationships, livelihood, skills, survival. Some of them are choices. Some, including many we'd call choices, are compromises. Some are accidents. None of them is [my] identity."[7] A better list, which can help me form a mission statement for the future, would include "what I do with energy and joy . . . what I love."[8] A little history is in order then. After that, we'll move on to see where we can find these more impactful motivators in our future.

What *Did* You Do?

Let's start at the beginning. On the lines below, fill in as many of the jobs you've ever had as you can remember. Don't worry about formal titles or organization names, just list what you've done and be as complete as possible.

For example, my list would look something like this:

> Babysit, sell ice cream at the beach, write, drugstore clerk, operate a fiberglass punch press, waitress, write, deliver newspapers, waitress, write, check in books, answer reference questions, supervise a department, be a library administrator, teach, be a speaker, plan events, write, teach classes, offer keynote speeches, write.

What about you? What did you do?

_____

_____

_____

_____

_____

Next, it's time to get not just nostalgic, but a bit more reflective. Take another look at your list and, of all the things you've done, what parts of them . . . what activities, what intentions, what contributions did you most enjoy? What parts did you love? As a further example (and because, realistically, I want to go through this renewal, too!), my reflection would include:

> I loved writing, anywhere for any purpose. I loved to teach because it helps others to grow and succeed. I loved to organize and lead events and to have the opportunity to create and develop new ideas.

How about you? Of everything you listed above that you've done . . . what have you loved? (We'll call this LIST A.)

_____

_____

_____

_____

_____

What *Do* You Do Now?

Fast forward to today. You need to be able to answer "Are you being or doing anything that resembles (what you love) now? If so, what (are You doing?) And, if not, why not?"[9] Through this examination of how you are currently spending your energies, talents, and days, it will be much easier for you to recognize what to focus on and the best parts to let go, as you move forward.

In the course of an average week, list everything—all the work—you do *now*, both inside and outside of your "job."

_____

_____

_____

_____

_____

Now comes the hard part. Of everything on that list . . . you're going to need to identify what parts of it you *love*. Please don't confuse this question with *what are your strengths,* because that's an entirely different question. Surprised? It would seem that our strengths aren't what we always thought they were . . . that is, what we do well . . . but they are actually what we do that energizes and motivates us. "Your parents were wrong! But it wasn't their fault. Everyone has been taught that, in order to be successful, more productive, more well-rounded and happier we need to learn to overcome our weaknesses. But a 30-year research study tells us that's wrong. If you understand what your strengths are and spend most of your time playing to those you will actually be much more fulfilled and (studies show) successful."[10]

So, from your list of what you are doing now, how exactly can you tell what energizes you, what motivates you, *what you love*? How can you look back on that list of jobs and pick the ones that mattered the most? According to Marcus Buckingham, the author of *Now, Discover Your Strengths,* we can use the following questions[11] to look for honest answers. To rate your list above, look at each individual task or activity you've recorded and ask yourself:

Do you look forward to doing it?
When you're doing it, does time stand still?
After you've finished, do you feel great?

Describe below, then, from your *what you are doing now* list—what is it that you love? (We'll call this LIST B.)

_____

_____

_____

_____

_____

What Would You *Love* To Do?

You've considered both what you did and what you're doing now...so move forward and think about your dreams, hopes, and (soon to be) plans. Is there something missing that you want to add to your days? Since the purpose of this book is to help you get excited about your future, you need to pick a path and chart a course that truly matters and feel, finally, refreshed and *renewed* to follow it. It's exciting, isn't it, to realize there are going to be some changes to how you spend those twenty-four most precious gifts each day...your time.

It's Easier to Fall Backward Than Forward

Be careful as you begin this journey. Sometimes, when our realities get in the way of our dreams, it's easy to return to comfortable (if not rewarding), recognized patterns, even if they're to be found in uncomfortable and uninspiring surroundings. It's actually quite common to find some people stuck in jobs that are actually making them physically sick, mainly because that option is easier than searching, reaching, and changing to try something new. Put very simply, it's easier, when falling, to fall backward than forward.

But *easy* isn't renewal, *easy* is often a rut.

When you think about your days in terms of your now-clarified values and mission, it's easy to see that there's plenty of room for excitement and challenge, even if you end up staying and growing right where you are. This is because it's not *where you are* but where you've been and *where you're going* that makes a career—and a person—a success.

In other words, it's not the standing still but the constant growth that helps us continually develop and our lives continually unfold. That's why that guy next to you, the one they say has *plateaued,* is so miserable! He's stuck.

This is only chapter 2, but I'm going to already give away the *most critical secret* to success . . . in *any* job, in *any* career, at *any* stage and in *any* life—and that secret is to stay in motion.

"In today's job market, you have to reinvent yourself to stay competitive by turning your current skills into new and different positions. Instead of starting all over again, you can start by building on what you already know."[12] If this is starting to sound hard, that's because it is.

Why bother, then? What's the point of work? Why struggle to make sure that your values match your work so that the result is something that matters? Since, "you're probably going to spend about 90,000 hours working"[13] in your lifetime, it certainly seems worthwhile not to "go days or years on cruise control"[14] but to make sure your mind . . . and work . . . "is stretched to its limits in a voluntary effort to accomplish something difficult—and worthwhile!"[15]

In a workshop I often teach about motivation and career directions, I begin by asking attendees to create a list of ten responses to the question, "Why do you work?" Then, to really get to the point, I ask them to write down ten more answers to "Why do you work *hard?*" The difference in motivators is amazing.

In order to find and clarify whether you're in a place right now that can fully support the future you desire, ask yourself *are you just working, or are you working hard* and why? Are you giving all you can give? A clear sign of commitment and dedication to your work is giving 110 percent to what you do. But how can you really tell if that's what you're doing . . . or if you're just on cruise control? Let's use some questions[16] from performance strategist Laura Garnett to help clarify what *working hard* might mean to you and to your future.

1. *No matter where you are, when you think about your work, do you feel energized?* Garnett says this means you wake up excited, thinking about what you're doing at work. This is what I've always called a *Sunday Night* test. I've seen people who absolutely hate their jobs and, as a result, they hate Sunday nights. On the contrary, some of us actually wish the weekend would hurry up and end, so we can get back to work! Interesting. How about your job? How does it make you feel, even on Sunday?

2. *Are you just a little nervous and challenged by all you have to do?* If your "To Do" list is overwhelming, but not terrifying, then you are one of the lucky ones who can use challenge as a motivator.

3. *Do you spend more time doing your work or daydreaming about someone else's job or what you want to do next?* People in this category are *always* reading the classifieds, or waiting for the weekend, or waiting for their summer vacation, or waiting for retirement, or waiting to die. Okay, maybe this is an exaggeration. Still, some people truly hate work that much. And that can tell you all you need to know. Time for that group to move on!

4. *Does everything just feel right—that you're doing something valuable and making an impact?* In this case, you and others can actually *see* that what you are doing matters (and you really don't care if they see it or not) and it feels really good. My example of this comes from the three years I spent as a reading tutor for two illiterate adults. While I've had the privilege of doing a lot of wonderful, meaningful things in my life, absolutely nothing has felt as good as that did.

5. *Do you feel like you're no longer on your way . . . you're there? You feel successful.* You don't compare yourself to others. Rather, you measure your intent, actions, and impact against your own personal and professional values—and you're happy with the result.

Garnett summarizes what these five realities can tell us by explaining, "While it's not realistic to spend every waking moment at high-octane performance, it is realistic and possible to be tapping into your talents and purpose. When you experience the above, you know how exhilarating work and life can be. If you are not, then it may be a wake-up call to know that there is more you could be getting out of your professional life."[17]

The Secret Formula: Values + Mission = Action

So how do you go about finding what that *more* is? Considering, studying, contemplating, and finally understanding what energizes (and what deflates you) is critical to your renewal process. These are not simple concepts, nor is the process of applying them to your own future an easy one. So, at this point, let's be crystal clear how you can recognize the strengths and skills that can carry you forward into your future. Just follow the SIGNs.[18]

S = SUCCESS

You can "feel" success when you do certain things. You feel in control and effective, like you have accomplished something good. Which parts of the work you love make you feel that way?

_____

_____

_____

_____

_____

I = INSTINCT

We know when we're about to have fun or to be happy. We can just tell. We can't wait, we anticipate the opportunity with excitement. That's our instinct. Which parts of the work you love make you feel that way?

_____

_____

_____

_____

_____

G = GROWTH

When we grow our skills and our energies we feel so focused that we often don't even recognize time passing. Which parts of the work you love affect you that way? What do you do at work that, when you look up and see that the day is almost over, you wish it weren't?

_____

_____

_____

_____

_____

N = NEEDS

Our physical need to (phew) take a break and rest comes after we've finished something that's truly fulfilling. What work do you do that wipes you out—in a good way—like that?

_____

_____

_____

_____

_____

Remember, values + mission = action. Read your signs carefully. For now, try to identify just one common theme. Next year, you might just be up for another renewal, but for the purposes of this book and this process, start with a single focus.

Your Renewal Plan: Step Two—What?

Select the most moving, most important, most compelling theme you see and complete the sentence below, then copy your answer onto Line #4 in *Your Renewal Plan* in the back of this book.

> Now that I see what really matters to me and where my strengths can help me make a difference, I'm going to find a way to get involved in the area of:
>
> 4. _____

Needless to say, you're going to want to select something you truly love doing in order to feel really renewed. After all, the whole point of this process is to get back to your passion. So go back and, once again, carefully review your Lists A and B and select three key areas in which you could bring your values alive. Write them below, then enter them onto Lines #5, 6, and 7 in *Your Renewal Plan* in the back of this book.

I can think of several ways I can do this, but to get the ball rolling, I'm going to seriously consider these three options and then, later, focus in on just one when it's time to set my first goal:

5. _____

6. _____

7. _____

Now you know who you are and you have a big-picture idea of what you want to do. The next question up is *when* is all of this going to take place? When is the right time to move forward—and how will you recognize it when it's here?

Night, Montreal[19]

The night is calm and a diamonded dust coats
the silent ship and me.
And what by day is so ugly, the coal dock,
wears the lunar litter too,
Like the coffle of circus elephants, sent from center ring, trunk and
tail coupling them, proud mahouts astride,
but back in my own world I make my round.
I enter the galley and leave it, cursing the offering from the urn,
A liquor no kin to coffee, a potion my kidneys would rush to void.
I checked the stern, all shipshape there.
I lean on the railing and spit white spit.
I hear a pulsing rhythm, the vast unrefined current easting to the
sea. And still the turns ply the river, going, coming,
I tell it from their cries.
But what do they seek in the water,
is it so gold a fish that it glows?
And where is the wind?
What fox does it chase that the smoke
climbs straight from the stack?

—WMH, DECKHAND, ARTHUR ANDERSON

NOTES

1. Richard N. Bolles, *How to Find Your Mission in Life* (Berkeley, CA: Ten Speed, 2000), 62.

2. Barbara H. Suddarth and David M. Reile, *Career Development Facilitator Curriculum Student Manual*, 3rd edition (National Career Development Association, 2012), 5.

3. William J. White, "From Day One: CEO Advice to Launch an Extraordinary Career," Pearson: Higher Education, 2006, https://www.pearsonhigher ed.com/samplechapter/0132206862.pdf.

4. John G. Miller, *QBQ!: The Question Behind the Question: What to Really Ask Yourself: Practicing Personal Accountability in Business and in Life* (Denver, CO: Putnam, 2004), 83.

5. "Why Does Your Work Matter?" *idonethis* blog, August 2014, http://blog .idonethis.com/why-does-your-work-matter.

6. "How to Make Work Matter," *Forbes*, forbes.com, March 9, 2014, http://1 .http://www.forbes.com/sites/meghanbiro/2014/03/09/how-to-make-work -matter/#46b4e4811ba9.

7. Barbara Sher and Annie Gottlieb, *BT-Wishcraft* (New York: Ballantine Books, 1983), 4.

8. Ibid, 5.

9. Laurie Beth Jones, "Inspiring Personal Growth: What Is Your USP?" Jones Group, in e-mail blog, June 11, 2015.

10. "Learn to Recognise Your True Strengths—Hint: They Aren't Just What You're Good at," Ignite Global, 1, http://igniteglobal.com/learn-to-recognise -your-true-strengths-hint-they-arent-just-what-you-are-good-at/.

11. Ibid.

12. "Do You Know Your Skill Set?" AARP Foundation, Worksearch Information Network, www.aarpworkscarch.org/RESEARCH/Pages/JobsinDemand.aspx.

13. Laura Garnett, Inc.com, June 2016, http://1.http://www.inc.com/laura -garnett/5-signs-that-youre-maximizing-your-potential.html.

14. Ibid.

15. Ibid.

16. Ibid.

17. Ibid.

18. Marcus Buckingham, "Know Your Strengths, Own Your Strengths," Leanin .org, http://leanin.org/education/know-your-strengths-own-your-strengths -no-one-else-will/.

19. Werner M. Hakala. "Night, Montreal," personal copy of poem, n.p., Ashtabula, Ohio, n.d.

WHEN IS THE TIME RIGHT?

Today is the first day of the rest of your life.
—Charles E. "Chuck" Dederich, Sr.

Dear Abby,
I've been a nurse for many years but I've always really wanted to be a doctor. I'm thinking of going back to medical school now, but I'm not sure it's the right decision. It will take me 5 years to become a doctor and, in 5 years I'll be 50! What should I do?

Signed,
Too Old to Start Over?

Dear Too Old to Start Over,
In 5 years you'll be 50 anyway, won't you?

Abby[1]

Timing Isn't Everything

Question: When is the right time to change your life?
Answer: By the end of this chapter, you'll know.

We make decisions every day. Good decisions, bad decisions, lukewarm decisions, unsuccessfully avoided decisions. The problem is, every time something bad happens as a result of our decisions, we're left a little more fearful of making the next one. Why? Because it's in our nature to focus on the negative. "Unless we are occupied with other thoughts, worrying is the brain's default position."[2]

And that, in a nutshell, is probably why it can take so long to renew.

Think back to when you made your very first life or career decision: was it the right time to do so? How about the tenth one you made, or yesterday's? "Here's the deal: There's no such thing as the wrong decision. There's simply the decision you make. You can weigh the pros and cons for eons. You can call your friends, your psychic, and the angel card reader. You can literally spend your entire life debating. You can miss shining opportunities because you were paralyzed by your fear of getting it wrong. You can watch your life pass before your eyes by trying to avoid getting it wrong. You can stay exactly where you are forever because you're afraid of getting it wrong. Or you can move forward."[3]

When you move forward isn't half as important as *that* you move forward. Even on the winding paths that are our careers, we can all reflect on the brass rings we missed or the wrong ones we grabbed, or we can focus on now—and why today is the right time to try again. The truth is, even in failure, we've moved forward and even while misstepping, we have grown.

Timing isn't everything. Action is.

When Does Success Begin (and Will You Recognize It When You See It)?

As much as we'd like to believe it, most of us are not the beautiful girl sitting at the soda fountain counter, who is about to be discovered and made into a Hollywood star; nor are we the lonely housewife who is about to casually pen an award-winning romance novel. More common knowledge tells us that "it takes 20 years to make an overnight success."[4] Or maybe even more. So most of us are on a journey that is being steered by two indisputable truths: (1) we might as well enjoy ourselves along the way, and (2) we're never really done.

There have been times in the past that weren't prime for career growth or for following dreams. Indentured servants were locked into their futures. Often working for years, or even a lifetime, to pay back a debt, they had no options for realizing or even enjoying their life's work. Apprentices in the early twentieth century also threw in their lot with a single profession—and were stuck there, successful or not. And Hermey, that special elf from *Rudolph the Red-Nosed Reindeer,* just wanted to be a dentist.[5] But he made it finally, didn't he? So there's hope for the rest of us yet, as long as we realize that while timing is not in our hands, our time is.

Meet Anna, Successful Writer

You may be thinking this all sounds great, but, still, this just isn't the right time to follow your dreams and make the kind of contribution you really want to make. At least, not with the job you currently have and all the responsibilities weighing on you. Rather, right now you should just stick with what you're doing and be satisfied that, some day, you can be truly happy. How's that working out for you?

Maybe Anna's story can convince you that *anytime* can be the right time.

But there's one very important reality to understand first. You don't have to do it all at once. A journey of a thousand miles begins with a single step.

You see, renewing your commitment to your own happiness and fulfillment does not always require a major life change. You don't have to (necessarily) quit your job, move away, or certainly avoid all your other responsibilities. The trick lies in finding out how to make *every* moment in your life the right moment to take just one step—or maybe two—towards where and what you want to be.

- Don't wait until your situation is perfect. It likely never will be, but that's okay.
- Don't wait until other people agree with you. Some opposition will always be normal.
- Don't wait until the skills you need are perfect. You'll learn more and build better skills by doing, rather than by waiting.[6]

For most of us, we will bounce throughout our lives and careers from one job—chosen for the right or wrong reasons—to the next. But at every step along the way, we can be moving closer to our real purpose. By finding a way, no matter how small, to stay focused on our true values throughout our journey, we can actually be following a path toward success. Remember, it's not the curves in the road that count, it's being willing to take them and hang on that matters.

The truth is, for every step we take, we're going to have to learn to take the good with the bad. And that goes for all the jobs we accept as well. Although they may not seem so at the time, the *bad parts* are usually superficial (it's too hot or cold or dirty, it's not fun, the commute stinks, the pay is worse), while the *best parts* (what we can accomplish) are what can continually move us forward.

So, here's the story. Anna (not her real name) is a writer who is as successful as she wants to be. Her story of rotten jobs, career missteps, and squandered and invisible opportunities can tell us a lot about how to make *when* our *now*, no matter where we are in life. Because at every stage of her life, she somehow found a way to pursue her mission. . .

The one thing Anna knew for sure was that she always loved and valued words, books, thoughts, and stories, from as far back as she could remember. She didn't want to become a writer; she was a writer. Even if it didn't always look that way . . .

Ah, Childhood

Anna loved going upstairs (rarely allowed) in her grandmother's house and sneaking into her uncle's room. Off to one side, in what used to be a closet of sorts, he kept an old-fashioned, manual typewriter and all of his writing utensils. You could smell the ink and paper as soon as you walked into the small room. There were also multicolored pens, lots of paper, pencils, erasers, and scribbled first drafts all over the table. As a small child, she might have been too young to know what it all meant—that her uncle was a writer—but the signs were there . . . she was one, too! (To be continued . . .)

Can young children seem to pick their chosen vocation at such an early age? And, if so, how does that usually happen? Often, it is due to the impact that an older, much-loved relative has. Or, minus the love, the power of a domineering adult influencer. Jeanette Mulvey tells us that "the way a child turns out can be determined in large part by the day-to-day decisions made by the parents [or other influential adults, ed.] who guide that child's growth."[7] How? Mulvey explains:

- Parents can initiate our trajectory, based on either the parents' preferences or observations of the child's characteristics and abilities.

- Parents might sustain our progress using encouragement and praise [and what child doesn't seek that from their Mom and Dad? ed.].
- Parents even influence our progress by modeling desired behavior and controlling our experiences.[8]

Ask yourself this . . . how many lawyers, teachers, doctors, or military people do you know whose children have followed in their footsteps? Surely, those people who are important to us as kids have a strong impact on charting our future.

But what else can steer us early on? While this section is not intended to blame the parents for our missed dreams, there's a bit more that happens early on at home that research has proven has a lot to do with the professional choices we later make.

Writing about how birth order can impact our lives and choices, Rachel Zupek quotes Michael Gross, author of *Why Firstborns Rule the World and Last Borns Want to Change It*, who claims that "a child's position in the family impacts his personality, his behavior, his learning and ultimately, his earning power."[9] See if you can find yourself in her further descriptions:

- *Firstborns* tend to pursue vocations that require higher education.
- *Middle Kids*, the peacemakers in the family, tend to end up in jobs that require negotiating and people skills.
- *The Babies of the Family* are used to the limelight. They often gravitate towards working in art, in creative endeavors, or out of doors.
- *Only Children*, not to be forgotten, are even more motivated to conform to parental expectations and often end up, no matter where they work, as achievement-oriented perfectionists.[10]

With all of these influences converging on our small, unassuming childhood personalities, it's no wonder some of us often end up steered (with all good intention) light years away from our own true values! Still, if you think back to Anna's secret trips to that *writing closet* of her youth, we see that it is possible, on our own, to feel the tug of those driving forces that will ultimately make up who we are. Sometimes we're even lucky enough to realize them, whether from the beginning, middle, or end of our careers.

"Even as a child, Tim Lopez remembers wanting to be a firefighter. 'I was a kid and I lived in town and I was just amazed at how every time the sirens went off, the guys would run out of their businesses, jump on the trucks as volunteers to fight the fires,' said Lopez. 'I swore than someday I would become a volunteer firefighter.' ... Lopez did just that."[11] And this single example is not the exception ... but often the rule.

So, in retrospect, what was the *best part* that Anna took away from those early, stolen glimpses of the life of a writer? She would suggest it was that she began early on to realize her passion for the written word. To some, that upstairs closet might have just looked like a place to store a bunch of blank pieces of paper and a big, scary machine, but to her those items were home to a writer.

The Teen Years

Ah, high school. One blogger put it best when she wrote, "When I was a teen, I had grand dreams of becoming a famous voice star/singer/ writer/trapeze artist. But, considering I couldn't afford anything that wasn't free, I (my parents) decided I should get a job ... until the whole trapeze artist thing panned out."[12] Personally, I was committed to becoming a jockey for many years, until I reached a height of 5'8" in junior high. Dream over.

Here's the rub. While the good news is many of us actually did begin working in our teens in professions we're still in today, the bad news is we usually didn't do so because it was the job of our dreams. (If that were the case, we'd all be movie stars, astronauts, or veterinarians!) Far from selecting jobs based on our true values, we chose them in our teen years for much more practical reasons, such as location (especially if we didn't drive, they needed to be accessible), our schedule (anytime after school or on weekends, except when we were otherwise occupied), and experience (we didn't have any.)[13] Anna's story continues ...

In Anna's high school, everyone made fun of the English teacher. She was old (at least forty), graying, and always badgering the kids to live up to their potential—which really meant volunteering for extra work. To raise your hand in response to one of these invitations was to be a traitor to the curve and yet, the first time she asked for students who might want to write for the school newspaper, Anna found her hand up in the air. Before long, she was published. There it was, in black and white, her name and picture over the school's news column in the local paper. Ignoring the fact that she had to juggle homework and an after-school job as well, Anna found a way to fit something positive into those awkward years. For her, those few column inches were the best part of her teenage years.

On to College

There's a debate going on that's as old as the bee's knees, and we're no closer to settling it now than we ever were. Some say college students should work, but no more than "10 to 15 hours a week—and on campus."[14] Others say more than that is required, whether in their profession or out of it and either on campus or off, and still others maintain students shouldn't work at all but should spend all their time studying. Right. So how in the world are we supposed to make our first, great, professional career decisions based on all that conflicting advice?

Let's look at the realities that can drive college students to work first:

- They have to eat. Extra money, above and beyond today's spiraling tuition costs, can often mean the difference between food and, well, it's hard to study when you're hungry.

- Preparation for real-life budgeting. There's more to be learned while in college than just how to pass the final. Students who work and attend classes are more likely to be better prepared to manage their grown-up budget after their sheltered campus life is over.

- It's not what you know . . . it's who you know. Ask any group of adults how they got at least one of their best jobs and chances are it will be due to knowing the right people. Getting outside the dorm and the classroom to meet real professionals can help build a network that will last a lifetime.

- Balance. After four (or more) years of thinking that yours are the only priorities that matter, it might be difficult to successfully join a professional team and juggle multiple deadlines and expectations.[15]

Convincing arguments, maybe, but still easier said than done. And, should we decide (or be forced) to take the plunge into the working world in between classes, we're still pretty unlikely to be picking our dream job—and more liable to be taking whatever will fit into an already demanding schedule—and maybe even give us time to study on the payroll. The story continues:

Three part-time jobs, one on campus and two off, plus an average of five classes a semester made for some pretty full days for Anna. The first two years at college seemed to fly by in a kaleidoscope of alarm clocks, schedules, time cards, too small paychecks, and homework assignments (over)due. Yes, okay, and fun. Then, in the beginning of year three, she learned she was now allowed to work at the campus newspaper. Feeling that lifelong pull of her love of writing, all of a sudden everything else became secondary. Classes were selected not on their merit, but only if they didn't require consistent attendance (because she was likely to be chasing a story). Those part-time job work schedules were shifted to begin earlier (yes, there was such a thing as 7:00 a.m.), and end later (who needed to sleep anyway?), freeing up the middle of the day for reporting, editing, writing headlines, and schmoozing with the other journalists. After all, that was the best part of those four years!

An Early and Growing Career

Now, what? With that diploma in hand, life can quickly become a kaleidoscope of parties, resumes, rejections, suggestions, and prayer. Some might even argue that grad school is the most common reaction to graduation, simply because the alternative (working) is too daunting.

Kathie Lee Gifford got some sage advice from her father, who said, "'Honey, find something you love to do and then figure out a way to get paid for it.' He understood that where your true passion is, there your joy is also."[16] She then adds, "Make no mistake, it's never too late to start."[17]

But all too often we start, then restart, and then start again, always looking for that shinier brass ring and our true calling. While it's true that, at this stage of our careers, we are finally beginning to feel the freedom to follow our dreams, it's not always as easy as it sounds.

"'True calling' is a messy term, since (a) job mastery, (b) job satisfaction and (c) compensation don't always line up. There are talented, yet miserable investment bankers (a and c, not b), talented and fulfilled public school teachers (a and b, not c) and several shan't-be-named general managers of professional sports teams (b and c, not a)."[18]

There are plenty of reasons why young professionals have so much trouble finding that perfect fit in their early and developing careers. What those suffering from this malady need to realize is that it's all just part of the plan. Crushing as it may seem to not get that job you *really* wanted, it's true what your real friends will tell you—there's something better out there. But it's never easy to believe that "when things fall apart, they could actually be falling into place."[19] Still, let's consider two of the main reasons you may be a bit confused:

1. *You Don't Know What You Like*—If you don't know what you like, the opposite scenario occurs. Every job in the world becomes a possibility. Or perhaps you try to hit the moving target of today's coolest or most lucrative career paths. Your attention scatters and your attempts at developing a career suffer.

2. *You Know What You Like, But You Don't Think It's Okay*—Confusion can stem from the fact that what you want conflicts with what the people around you tell you is acceptable or possible.[20]

There is hope. Just a quick look at some of the more bizarre realities and career shifts experienced by some now-successful individuals can make even the most uncertain young adult confident that, some day, they'll find the right path to where they want to be. It may even come as a result of reading this book.

- At age 23, Tina Fey was working at a YMCA.
- At age 23, Oprah was fired from her first reporting job.

- At age 24, Stephen King was working as a janitor and living in a trailer.
- At age 27, Vincent Van Gogh failed as a missionary and decided to go to art school.
- At age 30, Harrison Ford was a carpenter.
- Grandma Moses didn't begin her painting career until age 76.[21]

This could explain the Japanese proverb, *fall seven times and stand up eight.* But, what happened to Anna?

A card-carrying member of the 1970s feminist movement, Anna followed the Woodward and Bernstein movement and, overcoming all barriers in her way, clawed her way into a coveted writing job. Finally. And then it all fell apart. Well, it wasn't really that dire. The truth was, just as she felt she'd reached the pinnacle of her professional career, she was blessed with more than just a career—she was a young parent. So she hopped on the merry-go-round of job-jumping to find something that both met her professional values and goals and could take place in be-tween 2:00 A.M. feedings . . . and without the need for day care. Transla-tion? She waited tables. She sold retail. Then she waited more tables. But she was still a writer now, even if she wasn't—literally—writing, and, as life really began to happen for her, she found she had more and more to say. Anna's first novel was written, in large part, on the backs of paper place mats while on break. That was the "best" part of her early career—she finally had something to say!

Plateauing

And then there are the times when everything seems right—the job, the organization, the pay, but still something seems off. You're over it. Commonly called everything from burnout to plateauing, this stage of our career, more than perhaps any other, can be a clear signal that it's time for a renewal.

You still have lots to contribute, and your energy, skills, and in-tention are there but . . . something is just missing. Often, those closest to us can see this level even before we do. (That's what best friends are for.) But we can also watch for the signs and then commit to do something about them. *What* you will choose to do is, well, most likely finally up to you!

Signs You're Ready for a Major Life Change

- You're going through a life upheaval
- You're at the end of your rope—and you know it's now or never
- You're tired of merely surviving [or "just" working, ed.]
- Your current life is too small to fit your big dreams
- Your soul is calling you to be, have, and do more
- All signs point to *yes*
- You're reading this [book, ed.][22]

The Gold Watch Years

Retirement isn't for everyone. For some, it can be a depressing walk towards the reaper. For some, it can be a decision they didn't get to make and at a time when they didn't want to go. But, for many, it can be a flying carpet ride to *whatever I want to do* land.

If this is where you are right now, congratulations! If you've come to this juncture of your own accord, and you're anxious to get on with the business of realizing your dreams, bravo. Assuming that's the case, there will be no shortage of advice, good wishes, ideas, and demands put on your time. *Don't agree to do anything! Just relax. Don't sit around. Stay busy!* Whatever choice you make, you can pull it off successfully by keeping these nuggets of advice in mind (all of which, I must say, point directly at a healthy and positive renewal).

- *Find your passion.* [Or get it off the shelf and dust it off, ed.]
- *Take a leap of faith*—and find out who you really are.
- *Create a success inventory*—and celebrate all you've already accomplished.
- *Push back against the limits you've set for yourself.*
- *Add new tools to your belt.*
- *(Consider) retirement not an end, but a new beginning.*[23]

Here's how the story ends:

Anna is retired now. She writes during the mornings and volunteers, reads, and relaxes in the afternoons. And whenever she wants to, she does a little of her old work, just to help out those new to their careers. In reflecting on her convoluted path to success, she cites a favorite quote that she always used as a bellwether at every stage . . . "You've only got one real job you'll ever do, and that job is to live your whole life."[24]

The Life Cycle of Purpose

It's time to take a look back at your own path. No matter where you worked or didn't work or wished you had worked throughout your life so far, what was the best thing to come out of each situation? Were you able to fit in some piece of what you've always wanted to do? Did you burn the midnight oil, create sculptures on the weekend, or volunteer with disadvantaged kids on the weekends? List your *bests* below and then reread the list, and appreciate that your muse has always been in you somewhere.

WHEN *I WORKED AS A . . .*   *THE BEST THING THAT HAPPENED AS A RESULT WAS*

_____   _____

_____   _____

_____   _____

_____   _____

_____   _____

_____   _____

_____   _____

_____   _____

_____   _____

_____   _____

_____   _____

_____   _____

_____   _____

_____   _____

_____   _____

Knowing When It's Time

We all have a tendency to want to be sure we're in the right place at the right time, but how can we be? We can't. But you can be confident and inspired that you're heading in the right direction if you can always feel some element of growth or meaning or purpose—no matter how small—in everything you do. Or, joy. So *every* time is the right time. This chapter is designed to ask the question, *when should you renew?* Hopefully, it has succeeded at suggesting, *how about now?* But, it's you who has to be convinced. You may have been putting off for much of your life some element of work or art or contribution that is really and truly important. Don't worry about how you'll fit it in. We'll get to that. For now, just commit to putting your dreams and values back on the front burner—and doing it now. After all, you are the one who gets to get up again tomorrow morning and do something, other than *just* work.

Your Renewal Plan: Step Three—When?

Commit by writing your decision below. Then, copy your realization onto Line # 8 in *Your Renewal Plan* in the back of the book.

It's time to do something *I* want to do. Keeping in mind the distractions (which I'll manage), challenges (which I'll respect but keep in perspective), or procrastination (which I will train myself to overcome), I'm going to make *this* the right time to make a change because:

8. _____

NOTES

1. "Dear Abby," no date available; personal recollection.
2. Ray Williams, "Are We Hardwired to Be Positive or Negative?" PsychologyToday.com, 1991, https://www.psychologytoday.com/blog/wired-success/201406/are-we-hardwired-be-positive-or-negative.
3. "There's No Such Thing as the Wrong Decision," Kate Northrup, "Entrepreneurship," February 24, 2016, http://katenorthrup.com/theres-no-such-thing-as-the-wrong-decision/.
4. "Eddie Cantor Quotes at BrainyQuote.Com," BrainyQuote, 2001, www.brainyquote.com/quotes/quotes/e/eddiecanto309843.html.
5. Paul Bedard, "Rudolph's Pal 'Hermey the Elf' Gets His Dentist's Degree after 50 Years," *The Washington Examiner*, November 20, 2014, www.washingtonexaminer.com/rudolphs-pal-hermey-the-elf-gets-his-dentists-degree-after-50-years/article/2556397.
6. Donald Latumahina, "Achieving Your Dream: How to Take the First Step," Lifehack.org, http://1.http://www.lifehack.org/articles/productivity/achieving-your-dream-how-to-take-the-first-step.html.
7. Jeanette Mulvey, "Parents May Have Big Impact on Career Choices," LiveScience, December 3, 2010, http://1.http://www.livescience.com/9059-parents-big-impact-career-choices.html.
8. Ibid.

9. "Can Birth Order Determine Your Career?" CNN.com, October 2008, http://1.http://www.cnn.com/2008/LIVING/worklife/10/22/cb.birth.order .career/index.html?iref=24hours.

10. Ibid.

11. Michael Kirby, "Since Childhood He Knew He Wanted to Help Others," AuburnJournal.com, September 19, 2008, http://1.http://www.auburn journal.com/article/childhood-he-knew-he-wanted-help-others.

12. "21 Best Part-Time Jobs for Teens and High School Students–Localwise," Localwise, *Get a Job!*, January 30, 2016, https://www.localwisejobs.com/ blog/21-best-part-time-jobs-for-teens-and-high-school-students/.

13. Ibid.

14. Laura W. Perna, "Understanding the Working College Student," AAUP.org, May 3, 2013, http://1.http://www.aaup.org/article/understanding-working -college-student#.Vyo8aBUrKCQ.

15. "Career Planning: Should Your Student Work Part-Time during College?" UniversityParent, http://1.https://www.universityparent.com/topics/career -planning/should-your-student-work-part-time-during-college-2/#gsc .tab=0.

16. Charles Grodin, *If I Only Knew Then . . . : Learning from Our Mistakes* (New York: Springboard, 2007), 63.

17. Ibid.

18. Thorin Klosowski, "Why It's Worth Job Hopping in Your 20s," Lifehacker, November 5, 2014, http://lifehacker.com/why-its-worth-job-hopping-in -your-20s-1655008192.

19. Regina Brett, *God Is Always Hiring: 50 Lessons for Finding Fulfilling Work* (New York: Grand Central Publishing, Hachette Book Group, 2015).

20. "The 2 Biggest Reasons You Can't Decide on a Career Direction," Brazen .com, November 1, 2012, http://1.http://www.brazen.com/blog/archive/ career-growth/the-2-biggest-reasons-you-cant-decide-on-a-career-direction/.

21. Allison Shaw Caldwell, May 2, 2016, https://www.facebook.com.

22. Lamisha Serf-Walls, "7 Signs You're Ready for a Major Life Change," HuffingtonPost.com, May 9, 2015, http://1.http://www.huffingtonpost.com/ lamisha-serfwalls/7-signs-youre-ready-for-a-major-life-change_b_7225108 .html.

23. "10 Secrets to a Successful Retirement," Next Avenue, "Retirement & Estate Planning," August 13, 2012, www.nextavenue.org/10-secrets-successful -retirement/.

24. Barbara Sher, *I Could Do Anything If I Only Knew What It Was* (New York: Dell, 1994), 176.

WHERE SHOULD YOU BE?

And remember, no matter where you go, there you are.

—Confucius

Right Place, Right Time

I think it's safe to assume that some people who picked up this book are looking for advice on how to quit their jobs. Their inspiration to change their lives comes more from wanting to escape an unhappy situation than from simply wanting to fulfill their dreams. That's okay because, who knows, that just might be what it takes.

But for many, doing something else, anything else, that feels more fulfilling and rewarding can come from anywhere, including from where you are right now.

So, where? Here or there? It's time to explore *where* your renewal should take place.

Hopefully, by now, you're now really excited to know finally what you *really* want to do with your life and you're ready to make a commitment to start *today*. But you may still be wondering if you can make any difference or improvement from where you stand right now. That can be a tough call and, as a result, it's where most of us get stopped in our tracks.

At this age (no matter what *this* age happens to be), we ask ourselves *where should I be in life?* With time running out, where can I start doing what I want to do? Am I in the right place to make a change? Should I quit my job and move to the Yukon? If I stay here, can I really make any changes for the better? Should I give up sleeping and just live two lives? Your answer to these questions involves a decision. And, as you decided in the last chapter, it's decision time.

A little guidance wouldn't hurt. Let's be honest, do you really *hate* your job? Because, if so, changing jobs as part of your renewal is certainly something to consider. Or do you have an even bigger mystery to solve because, believe it or not, you actually *like* where you are now . . . it's just somehow not enough . . . you just want *more*. What if you're one of those people who have a mixture of both dilemmas, so you *really* can't decide which way to turn?

With all of these possibilities in play, many people end up deciding this is just too big of a decision to make right now and, instead, they'll work on it "later. The problem is, later never seems to come and we keep putting off making the hard choices. None of us will live forever, and we're not guaranteed a moment past right now. Today is the day to claim the life you truly deserve."[1]

Although you could spend years examining every single aspect of these questions (they call that therapy), for the purposes of this step of your renewal, let's just drill down to the two most obvious possibilities and look at why they occur and some options if they have. Try to find yourself in these examples, then, and consider your options carefully. Hopefully, the right path will become clearer to you as a result.

Stay or Go?

In no particular order of importance, presented next are the "Top Ten" most common explanations I hear that drive people to either stay at their current job or leave. In order to be prepared to truly commit to those values you identified—and feel better about getting out of bed each morning—it's going to help for you to be comfortable with whichever choice you make. As you probably expected to hear, with all of these factors there are options. Sorry, but nothing can be so cut and dried. How you can or can't make your situation work is going to be up to you. There may be good reasons to stay and work to improve your current situation or to leave and search for a better fit. Consider them all, then try to decide where your *where* is.

Culture

I once knew a young man who was such a staunch vegan that he had to quit his lucrative waiter's job because he just couldn't stand serving the meat dishes. Couldn't do it. Or consider the feminist who was offered a high-paying marketing position with a country club that didn't allow female members. Wouldn't work. "If you are morally misaligned with your employer or you feel there are moral or ethical differences"[2] that you just can't overcome, then there's probably not much you can do to avoid a very "uncomfortable workplace setting."[3]

When teaching a graduate management class the keys to understanding and then selecting a workplace culture that matches their needs, I've often described that concept as the *personality* of an organization. Is it a safe place to work? Are employees respected? Encouraged? Is there trust or fear among the staff regarding their futures? And, most importantly, how can you tell?

Take trust, for example. Without it, people live in fear of doing something wrong and losing their jobs. This diminishes or even eliminates innovation, risk-taking, and learning. "In many organizations, employees are fired for errors. [At IBM in the 1960s], after an employee made a mistake that cost the company $10 million, he walked into the office of the CEO, expecting to get fired. 'Fire you? I just spent $10 million educating you!'"[4] Now that's a culture to stick with!

Options

While there's a lot about any organization that staff *can* change—given the right opportunities to speak up, offer alternatives, and provide sound arguments—the overall culture of a place is probably least likely to be one of them. You can try, of course, to show the benefit of providing a space safe for ideas, taking chances, and developing skills, but depending on how far apart you and your employer are on creating the right environment for success, this may be a tough nut to crack.

Money

"In the past, many companies relied on money almost exclusively to motivate their workforce, but employees often rate other aspects, such as recognition and flexibility, as more important."[5] Still, we gotta eat!

Referring yet again to Maslow's infamous hierarchy of needs (because I know you've heard this before), money seems to find its way into both the first and second levels of our need pyramid. "Physiological needs are requirements for human survival."[6] These include food, clothing, and shelter, all of which cost money. Once we have those taken care of, we look for security, including the financial kind.[7] So, yeah, money matters, but how much is enough? For example, I've not been able to find anywhere that Maslow talked about three-car garages, satellite television, or imported cars.

In other words, as hard as it might be to hear this, "money isn't everything and you're only worth what someone will pay you."[8]

Options

"Pay is negotiable, and good employers will listen to your salary concerns even if they can't afford to give you a raise. Talk to your boss about why you feel underpaid, and what it would take to make you feel adequately compensated."[9] Even though you may be able to prove that others in your same position are making more, this tactic may or may not work. Especially in nonprofits, there's only so much money to go around. But if the job is otherwise satisfying to you, it's certainly worth a try. If this doesn't work, don't just stay and be mad. "Unsatisfying pay makes you dread your daily responsibilities because you are painfully aware of the underwhelming reward for dong them."[10]

The Boss

Here's a very interesting truth that anyone who is a boss or (even more importantly) who supervises bosses needs to know. "A study came up with this surprising finding: If you're losing good people, look to their immediate supervisors. More than any other single reason, he [or she?] is the reason people stay and thrive in an organization. And he's the reason they quit. 'People leave managers not companies,' write the authors Marcus Buckingham and Curt Coffman. 'So much money has been thrown at the challenge of keeping good people—in the form of better pay, better perks and better training—when, in the end, turnover is mostly a manager issue.'"[11] How do you feel about your boss?

There's a lot to consider here, aside from obvious personality conflicts. Just as we aren't required to *like* our coworkers, we don't need to be best buddies with the boss, but we do need (and want) to have at least a bearable, professional level of mutual respect. The emphasis here is on mutual. Great bosses motivate, encourage, help, and develop employees. They're not just in it for the money, power, or prestige. Similarly, great bosses know what they're doing and what we should all be doing. They both lead and jump in when needed, if that's what it takes to get the job done.

It's easy to spot the fakes. One might be "a company president who takes his turn fielding calls on the switchboard throughout the year. He's one of us. [Then there's the] executive who doesn't let anyone use his parking spot—even when he's on vacation."[12] He's one of the *others*. The only way you can decide which you have and how hard they are to take is by your own personal measure.

Options

While it's true that leaving a job because of a terrible boss is often a good enough reason to go, before you go consider finding some ways to improve the relationship. You have rights and they should be written down somewhere. And *everyone* has a boss, even your boss. If it's possible for you to attempt a face-to-face conversation about your issues—and nothing is resolved—consider whether her or his superiors might be of help. As long as you offer solutions that focus on supporting the organization's mission, you've got nothing to lose.

Other times, these strained relationships can cause real damage, leaving you physically sick, stalling your career, or even pushing you out of a job.[13] You might not want to wait around to let any of that happen.

Talents

In a room full of brand-new supervisors who have gathered to learn how to do their job well, the conversation usually begins by thinking back to the best bosses they ever had and asking, what made them great? More often than not, the answer is that they helped others to shine. We all bring talents to our jobs. If we're lucky, those talents don't just get used, they get cultivated, stretched, tested, and developed. Or not.

"In an ideal job, you'll face slight challenges—tasks and initiatives that are slightly outside of your skillset and encourage you to reach new heights—almost every day. If you don't find yourself challenged, you'll feel bored and resentful and you'll grow to hate your job entirely."[14]

If you've been passed over for promotion, have not been offered the challenging assignments, and are no longer invited to the key meetings,[15] you may be starting to pick up on the fact that that your talents are not being fully used or, worse, that no one seems to care about what you have to offer. The resulting frustration and even resentment may just push you over the edge and send you looking for more.

Options

As long as everything else about your current job is great, you always have the option of assuming responsibility for your own growth. Remember the young librarian who rashly decided to stop training just because her library wouldn't pay her way? It didn't take her long to realize she was punishing (and limiting) herself with that conclusion. Once she realized it was *her* career after all, she decided to take vacation days, pay her own way, and continue to improve her skills. The result? She was later recognized not only for her expanded professional expertise, but also for her initiative, determination, and personal responsibility.

If this is the path you decide to take, just be certain that the resentment resulting from your limitations doesn't overtake your day-to-day performance. "If office politics is making it impossible for you to thrive, find a job where your talents ... and your potential ... will be recognized."[16]

Quitting a job is never a decision to be made lightly. As in any relationship, trial and error and a commitment to succeed should always be your primary options before you opt for throwing in the towel. If promotion or advancement is what you're looking for and you're certain "you can't get yourself any higher, try making a lateral move instead. Start developing peripheral skills or learning more about a different department. You'll add more skills to your skillset, increase your value as an employee, and refresh your perspective."[17]

After putting forth so much of yourself and seeing the results, the decision to stay or go that had looked so hard to make might not be so tough after all.

Vision

To be successful, organizations (and people) need to think strategically. Those who do it well actually write it down and then have a blueprint to follow to success. The key word here is success, because that's what we all ultimately want. Compare two organizations of your choice to confirm this. Pick one that is extremely successful. Everyone wants to work there. Articles or maybe even books are written about them. Future leaders study their processes and culture so as to mimic their achievements.

Next, study a similar organization, but one that is struggling to achieve its goals. Job openings stay open because, frankly, the workplace reputation is well known and doesn't exactly result in applicants clamoring at the door. Their funding is likely precarious, at best, and their impact is limited or perhaps even nonexistent.

The difference? It's usually the clarity of their vision, or lack thereof. It's worth repeating that people just want to be successful at what they do. They want to know their time, effort, and the sweat of their brow are making a difference. They want the confidence to make decisions and take actions without having to get permission, because the outcome is clear—and aligned with the organization's purpose. Without that clear direction, no one knows exactly what to do and we go from looking like a well-run organization with everyone on track to succeed to resembling, as one library manager so aptly put it, "a bunch of monkeys with a new red ball."[18]

A lack of overall vision and the resulting lack of organization and direction it provides can do a lot of damage, some of it serious enough to result in heavy staff turnover. Why?

- If employees don't have a clear sense of [the] company's mission, values, and vision, how can they carry them out? Disorganization will most certainly stifle a productive workforce.

- If a worker is unproductive, he or she is most likely disengaged. And disengaged employees decrease overall employee morale.

- Clients and customers can and will notice disorganization, which is an immediate red flag. How you run your business will show the client how you will ultimately handle the services/products you're providing.[19]

Options

You're going to need a purpose in order to motivate yourself to succeed. If that purpose isn't being provided by your organization, consider creating your own. Career experts advise professionals to set and annually reexamine personal goals (as you've been doing), so that you can keep yourself motivated and feel a personal sense of accomplishment.

At work, consider volunteering to lead an effort to clarify the mission, values, vision, and strategic directions that can help assure organizational success—and support.

Without either option, since you now know what you want to do, it might just be time to find an organization whose intent matches your own.

Passion

There's the work we *do* and then there's the work we *love*. The difference is that the latter fulfills our passion, while the former just pays us. You've already heard the old quote: "Choose a job you love, and you will never have to work a day in your life."[20] If it were only that easy, you might be thinking. Well, maybe it is.

People have been known to stay in jobs that offered little in the way of pay, prestige, or perks just because they were passionate about the work they were doing. Think ministers . . . or librarians! On the contrary, we read all the time about people who leave high-paying, impressive positions for the simpler life, which offers them a chance to follow their hearts.

Consider the story of Trent Hamm, creator of the popular website "The Simple Dollar." "In March 2008, I walked away from a great job into a writing career path that, at the time, paid me about 50% of what I was making at my previous job. To a lot of people in my life, this seemed like an amazingly difficult step. Why would I possibly make this move?"[21] As it turns out, the reasons involved a combined passion for what really mattered to him, including:

- Spending more time with family
- Grabbing what might be a one-time opportunity to write
- At least have a chance to earn more . . . down the road
- Do something that might actually help improve someone else's life[22]

Options such as these are often the most difficult to articulate, especially to those who will also be affected (read: family), and so they are overlooked and even ignored. But they shouldn't be. If we can't find a way to add passion for our work back into our days, then it truly might be time to look elsewhere. "Passion is what motivates people. To some extent, your job shouldn't feel like a job. If you can't think of any reason you would do your job other than receiving a paycheck, it's clear you've lost your passion [or you never had it in the first place]."[23]

Options

There are only two options. And for such a complex question, both can be answered by posing the question just mentioned. If you weren't getting paid, would you still choose to have your job? With that answer in hand, there are several choices you can make.

1. You could "try to rediscover what attracted you to the job in the first place. Look at your responsibilities from

a new angle, or find a new way to work that makes your job seem fresh.

2.   Alternatively, think about your true passions and how you can turn those into a new career."[24]

Security

When one man's small, family-owned company was purchased by a huge international firm, the writing was on the wall—changes were on the way and it wasn't going to end well. Then began the horrible days of waiting for the axe to fall—again and again. One by one (or, sometimes, even in twos or more) he watched his friends and longtime colleagues being walked to the door. Business pundits even came up with a cute acronym for the process . . . they calling it being *RIFFED* (stands for "reduction in force").

There's an immeasurable impact that stress has on us. It feels like worry, fear, uncertainty, and loss all rolled into one. That's why some people choose to leave where they are ahead of time; they simply can't stand the wait.

Options

"If you can stick it out until the economy picks up and the demand for your skill sets strengthens, you'd be better served"[25] by hanging around. Unless, of course, the uncertainly is doing horrible things to your life outside of work.

The question to consider, though, is what job is safe from the ambiguities of *job security* and what exactly does that promise? In today's ever-changing world, we all know deep down that "the job that's secure today could be gone tomorrow."[26] Just ask someone who planned on remaining a bank teller, cashier, newspaper reporter, or travel agent if they thought five or ten years ago that they had imagined all the workplace changes we've seen.

Your options, then, are to find security not in the name of your current company or organization or even in your title—but in yourself, your skills, your passion, and again, your Values. The chances are that those are elements of your character that will never go out of style.

Colleagues

For nineteen years, one staff member ate more meals with a particular coworker than she did with any of her family members. The connection between colleagues on the job is a close one—and a critical one. There is no shortage of people who have said they left a great job, with wonderful pay and lots of leadership vision and support, simply because they couldn't work another day with a specific (or even a group of) coworkers. Consider some possible reasoning to support this:

- When people know one another well, they are much more likely to work well together. (And, of course, the opposite can also be true.)

- Friendly coworkers look forward to being together when they do their jobs. And the resulting positive workplace feeling carries over to productivity and good morale. (Stiff, unfriendly, or intimidating places have the opposite effect.)

- When employees feel connected, not only to the organization but to their teammates, they're less likely to want to leave.

- Positive coworker relationships make for a productive workplace.[27]

So, no, you're not crazy to be thinking of leaving because you don't like your coworkers. It's perfectly normal to seek places to spend our time where we are comfortable and to avoid those where we're not.

Options

There's room for improvement in every situation and, as Gandhi once said, we can start by being the change we want to see. Face conflicts head on with professional communication. Seek compromises and mutual understanding of differences. Look for training or coaching opportunities to strengthen your team, beginning with yourself. Then, in the end, only you can judge whether there's hope for improvement or realize that some differences are just unresolvable.

Work/Life Balance

A quick scan of the available literature on work-life balance covers a multitude of research, including everything from brain functions on adequate sleep to romantic implications. Geez. And most thought it was just another trendy business catchphrase. Not so.

Although this seems to be one of the more difficult reasons to admit you're quitting, people are starting to put more and more stock in the realization that they can have it both ways—a great career and a happy family. Especially with today's two-party breadwinners, with technology supporting distance work and with a sharper awareness of the physiological implications of stress, people are demanding balance. How can you tell if it's missing? You can start with your health.

If your "work, people or culture are unhealthy . . . it has a negative impact on us physically and mentally."[28] For example, you might be:

- Gaining weight? Studies have shown that an unhappy work life robs you of the energy you need to make good dietary choices and to exercise.

- Feeling stressed? Workplace stress doesn't just come from being too busy at work or working too many hours; it's also a direct response to being in a state of negative affect while at work.

- How's your sex life? One of the worst things about hating your job is that it doesn't stop at the end of the workday. Researchers have found a clear link between a good relationship with your spouse and health.

- Having trouble sleeping? Frustrations can follow you home and then, if you're miserable at work, you might find it harder to fall asleep or just not sleep well at all.

- Do you get sick a lot? A study of unhappy nurses showed that they had a higher risk of being sick, and we're talking about serious diseases like cancer, heart disease, and diabetes.[29]

Another complication of negative work-life balance is that, quite obviously, since *life* is involved, the problems don't stop with you. Not being able to spend time with family, missing important family engagements, and simply not being *there* when you are home take a terrible toll on happiness.

Options

While you probably can't single-handedly change the operating culture of your workplace, you can try—before giving up entirely—to make some balance changes in your own corner of the world.

- Manage your time better. Carefully log and then evaluate what you do and see if you can reduce some things (especially those that cause you the most headaches). For example, supervisors are often the worst at keeping all the work for themselves. Although that doesn't sound particularly reasonable, it stems from not wanting or not knowing how to delegate. Take a course!

- Minimize technology, especially if it drives you nuts. Here's a question someone once asked in a time management course. If your mail delivery person came to your house every half-hour and put something in your mailbox, would you go out to get it every time? No? Then why do we allow our e-mail to take over our lives?

- Schedule open hours just for interruptions. Doctors do it and so do college professors. It's called office hours. When preparing your next day's activities, schedule in at least an hour when you're not expected to do anything. Then rest, think, take a walk, have a positive conversation, or undertake any other low-stress activity that won't get you fired . . . but will help you balance your energy throughout the day.

If none of these options are possible and you can't think of any other ways to enjoy both your work and your life, then you just might want to start looking for an employer who recognizes the value of that combination.

Attitude

In a book I wrote in 2011 (*Be a Great Boss: One Year to Success*), I started off by stressing the need for a positive attitude in the workplace. I noted that we should all seek and contribute to an attitude of "positivity, respect, support and encouragement."[30] I even shared an all-time favorite quote, "Attitude is your paintbrush. It colors every situation,"[31] to further emphasize how broad and all-encompassing this one characteristic can be.

And yet attitude may be the most pervasive reason given for people leaving their jobs. It's so basic. Respect—workers want to be valued, not talked down to and not overlooked or ignored. Opportunity—workers want (say again) to succeed, so that they can enjoy that heady sense of accomplishment that comes with a job well done. Kindness—enough said.

Of the ten possible reasons for quitting your job treated in this chapter, I have to say this one is the deal breaker, the watershed, the baseline requirement. Only you can take the temperature of the human attitude at your workplace. Value yourself enough to make it a critical measurement.

Options

Respect people, values, and contributions and expect others to do the same.

Starting Over

A word or two, before we move your renewal on, about *how* to leave if that is indeed what you eventually decide to do.

Before You Go

Although it may sound tedious, some of my favorite pieces of advice, along with these timeworn traditions of decision-making, should be critical final steps before making what could be the best—or the worst—decision of your career:

- Make a list. That's right. *Pro* on one side and *Con* on the other. Next list everything (maybe starting with this chapter) about what you like and what you don't like about your job. Consider all options and then ask yourself, will the answer that seems to be rising to the top allow my renewal to continue?

- Be like Spock. Do not let emotions get in the way of your decision. You've probably heard that people going through real-life crises, like death or divorce, are always cautioned not to make any big decisions at that moment. That's good advice, so sleep on it, at least.

- Leave a way back. One of my least favorite workplace rituals is the dreaded exit interview. Why? Because more bridges have been burned in this process than in the making of every war movie throughout history. This concept is rife with cliché opportunities (but that doesn't make them any less right). Bite your tongue. Take the high road. Turn the other cheek. Whatever you do or say before leaving, make sure it won't hurt *you* down the road, just in case you might want to come back.

- Have some other options on the table, or at least visible on the horizon.[32]

While You're Looking

You'll likely either be euphorically happy or dismally depressed when you wake up to realize you don't have anywhere to go. But while today's calendar might be empty, tomorrow's probably won't, so keep yourself ready to reenergize and move forward. In *Downgrade Your Job,*

Not Your Life, author Trent Hamm offers some really great tips for this *in-between jobs* stage:

- Live well below your means. That's one element of stress you *can* control.
- Pay down bills. Or better yet, eliminate as much debt as you can, especially if you just received a healthy severance package.
- Fill your spare time with doing what you love. (And, based on your values, you already know what that is.) Do this even as a volunteer, just for the satisfaction you will gain.
- Cultivate your *luck* by seeking opportunities. Connect with old friends. Strengthen and grow your network.[33]

What to Look *For*

Since you're committed to renewing yourself in every sense possible, make selecting where you will next work a part of that package. Now that you know for sure what you didn't like, make sure you don't settle for anything less than what you do like! How do you know if your next decision will be the right one? Have confidence in yourself, you now have:

- Clarity: Be brave about what you want, who you are, and what's important to you right now.
- Confidence: Win the battle of the brain (and that secret voice in your head) and trust yourself.
- Control: Nothing is holding you back now. It's your decision, so make it.[34]

Values Are Everywhere

This chapter is based on the premise that you're already somewhere. If you're not yet, maybe because you're a recent grad or someone just entering the job market, then these pluses and minuses should still be a great help in your decision-making.

I think, at this point, it's worth reviewing the Confucius quote that opened this chapter: "No matter where you go, there you are." In short, there is no perfect spot from which to begin your renewal. As a result, every spot can be perfect.

Your Renewal Plan: Step Four—Where?

Don't let your *where* decision slow you down. State now, by writing in the lines below, why where you are right now **is** the perfect spot from which to move forward.

Where I am right now is the perfect place from which to launch my renewal, because whether I decide to stay or to go, all things considered,

9. _____

Now, recopy your answer onto Line #9 in *Your Renewal Plan* in the back of the book.

Feeling a little nervous? That's natural. You're getting much closer to actually doing something about what's been in your heart for a long time. After piecing together all the elements currently in your life and committing to add even more, it's normal to become a bit overwhelmed. Couldn't you just get up tomorrow morning and keep doing the same thing? Sure, but, in the next chapter, a review of *WHY* you're doing all this will convince you that's not a good idea at all.

"Making a big life change is pretty scary. But, know what's even scarier? Regret."[35]

NOTES

1. Kimanzi Constable, "5 Signs You're Not Happy with Your Life (and What You Can Do About It)," HuffingtonPost.com, October 2, 2015, www.huffington post.com/kimanzi-constable/5-signs-youre-not-happy-with-your-life-and -what-you-can-do-about-it_b_8166980.html.

2. Jacquelyn Smith, "14 Signs It's Time to Leave Your Job," *Forbes*, September 4, 2013, www.forbes.com/sites/jacquelynsmith/2013/09/04/14-signs-its-time-to-leave-your-job/#4691a28e706f.

3. Ibid.

4. Adam Grant, "The One Question You Should Ask about Every New Job," Sunday Review, *New York Times*, March 28, 2016, www.nytimes.com/2015/12/20/opinion/sunday/the-one-question-you-should-ask-about-every-new-job.html?_r=0.

5. Scott Thompson, "The Importance of Non-Financial Rewards for the Organization," Small Business Chron 2016, http://smallbusiness.chron.com/importance-nonfinancial-rewards-organization-45146.html.

6. *Wikipedia*, 2016, s.v., "Maslow's hierarchy of needs," https://en.wikipedia.org/wiki/Maslow%27s_hierarchy_of_needs.

7. Ibid.

8. Amitai Givertz, "Should I Stay or Should I Go? 7 Arguments For and Against Leaving Your Job," Salary.com, www.salary.com/should-i-stay-or-should-i-go-7-arguments-for-and-against-leaving-your-job/.

9. "7 Reasons You Hate Your Job," Inc.com, "People," October 29, 2014, www.inc.com/jayson-demers/7-reasons-you-hate-your-job.html.

10. Ibid.

11. "Why Good Employees Leave?" David W Richard, TheLayoff.com, December 15, 2013, https://www.thelayoff.com/t/tbnQdtP.

12. Grant, "The One Question."

13. Givertz, "Should I Stay."

14. "7 Reasons."

15. Smith, "14 Signs."

16. Givertz, "Should I Stay."

17. "7 Reasons."

18. Patrick Jones, conversation, 1989.

19. Shala Marks, "4 Negative Effects of a Disorganized Company," Recruiter.com, August 12, 2013, https://www.recruiter.com/i/4-negative-effects-of-a-disorganized-company/.

20. Quote Investigator, September 2, 2014, http://quoteinvestigator.com/2014/09/02/job-love/.

21. Trent Hamm, "About," The Simple Dollar, 2016, www.thesimpledollar.com/about/.

22. Ibid.

23. "7 Reasons."

24. "7 Reasons."

25. Givertz, "Should I Stay."

26. Ibid.

27. Kate McFarlin, "Importance of Relationships in the Workplace," Small Business Chron 2016, http://smallbusiness.chron.com/importance-relationships-workplace-10380.html.

28. Smith, "14 Signs."

29. Alexander Kjerulf, "5 Signs Your Body Wants You to Quit Your Job," Care2, 2016, www.care2.com/greenliving/how-your-job-makes-you-sick.html.

30. Catherine Hakala-Ausperk, *Be a Great Boss: One Year to Success* (Chicago: American Library Association, 2014), 2.

31. Ibid.

32. Smith, "14 Signs."

33. "Downgrading Your Job, Not Your Life," The Simple Dollar, "Careers," March 1, 2011, www.thesimpledollar.com/downgrading-your-job-without-downgrading-your-life/.

34. Darcy Eikenberg, "To Stay or Leave Your Job? Four Secrets to Help You Decide," Red Cape Revolution, January 31, 2013, http://redcaperevolution.com/secrets-to-stay-or-leave-your-job/.

35. Lawrence, "Making a Big Life Change Is Pretty Scary. But Know What's Even Scarier? Regret," Tofurious Marketing Strategies for Smart Creatives, August 3, 2012, http://tofurious.com/quotes/making-a-big-life-change-is-pretty-scary-but-know-whats-even-scarier-regret/.

WHY BOTHER?

They always say that time changes things,
but you actually have to change them yourself.

—Andy Warhol

Why Not?

Hopefully, you are convinced by now that you are worth the effort it will take to renew at least some elements of your work and life. Because if you do make some changes, the resulting accomplishment will be well worth the effort. Consider who will benefit. How about you, your family, and your job. In short, everyone wins. And none of this improvement will necessarily require that you quit your job, desert your family, skip your car payments, or move to a hut on the beach and live under a palm tree.

Realistically, though, you just *might* end up looking for a new job or making some other, more reasonable changes, but that's all part of the process. The real goal you are moving towards can only be found within you. Once you've committed to somehow make more of a difference, even if it means making some big changes, you'll be surprised by *how* simple moving forward can actually be (we'll get to the *how* in the next and final chapter of this book.) Again, by refocusing, recommitting, and *renewing* promises you have been wanting to make to yourself for some time, you will end up feeling a lot better about your focus, your values, and how you spend your days.

If this is all starting to sound hard, then you're paying attention because it likely will be. Some people may even laugh at your attempts, or worse, predict your failure. The "f" word. Yikes. So *why* bother? *Why* take this on? *Why* try to be something you have never been (or maybe that you haven't been for a long time)? *Why?* Good question, but there's an even better one to start with.

Let's start by considering *why not.*

A former boss and invaluable mentor once suggested that when deciding to do a difficult thing, you should just ask yourself "What's the worst that can happen?"[1] as a result. If you can live with the answer, then do it!

So, let's answer *why not renew yourself* by saying out loud what just might be worrying you the most.

What's the Worst That Can Happen?

There are plenty of reasons to avoid a tough challenge. For many, those voices in our heads repeating well-intentioned (but limiting) parental advice are among the most influential. *Don't take risks. Make sure you have stability. Don't ever leave a job if you don't have another one lined up. Think of your responsibilities. Don't run with scissors.* Those are just a few of the many refrains that guide most of our early lives and careers. While there's no argument that it's important to be responsible and thoughtful when making important, life-changing decisions, they don't have to be mutually exclusive from what makes us happy, fulfilled, and challenged. If this makes sense, then why are we still so uncomfortable with risk and so, so afraid of the worst that can happen?

- We're afraid of the unknown and we *don't* like surprises!

  One thing to be said for the traditional job is that there are usually very few surprises. You can sit down with your kitchen calendar and chart your paydays with great relief and regularity, for example. You can also look ahead, see what opportunities for change and growth exist, and (usually) know what it will take to achieve them. Although the threats of layoffs, new skill requirements, and tornadoes do exist, chances are we're pretty safe if we just stay where we are, thank you very much.

- We are afraid to trust anyone to help us or to be involved in any way in our change.

I have a friend who consistently stays about 2–3 months behind in her rent. No problem. The landlord doesn't seem to mind a bit. Hmmm. I wonder if she will always have that landlord? Or, how about the person who passes up promotion after promotion because that would mean working for a different boss and she loves the boss she has—so she's staying. Hmmm. Wonder if her boss has committed to stay in her job forever? And what about the young married couple who assure each other that money doesn't matter—only happiness matters—so they take whatever positions suit their whim at the moment. Hmmm. Wonder what will happen to that relationship when the money runs out? There are other people involved in every decision we make, whether we like it or not. We either give too much or too little credit to the role they play in our risk-taking.

- Control is everything and we're afraid that without it, well, we just don't know what to expect.

  There's that issue of control again. This situation is a lot like why so many people are afraid to fly. When driving a car, we at least feel as though we'll be able to hit the brakes or turn the wheel away from a tree, but in that airplane we have *absolutely, positively, no question about it zero control. Zero.* There was a librarian who began her career in an entry-level position and virtually stayed in the same chair for thirty years. Such a shame and such a waste. She could have become a trainer or a mentor. She could have used the incredibly strong connections and relationships she'd built with community members to advocate for the library. She could have done so much more than just answer reference questions day in and day out, but if she'd branched out into any of those "new" options, she would no longer have been in control of her desk, her computer, her pens, her work space . . . her career. And that was just too scary because . . . she might have failed. And so she didn't risk it. In a lesson in true irony, even the chair she sat in became an object of immobility, as it was never allowed to be moved to a new spot or used by anyone else.

- No, timing is everything. In order to successfully manage a significant change, all the moons have to be aligned. In other words, the time must be right and we're afraid that the worst thing that can happen is we will pick the wrong time and everything will go downhill from there.

All she wanted to do was to get her career off the ground, but first there was the challenge of starting a family to consider. After returning to work, two more children came in quick succession, then evenings were reserved for homework, then parents and in-law concerns arose, and finally college visits demanded all of her extra time. Finally, her life was returned to her and, after being passed over for more than five promotions, she asked for some career advice. The time was perfect (for her) now and she wanted to know why in the world no one was willing to invest in the growth and development of someone only a handful of years away from retirement. Hmmmm.

Some people don't even like to move the furniture around. Others do that for fun. Many of us are afraid that if we take a chance and move, shift, alter, or somehow change something about our sturdy lives, then everything will fall apart like a Jenga game. How we feel about risk mirrors how comfortable we are with change in general (and whether or not we've worked on becoming more trusting and open-minded).

One woman stayed in a job she literally hated until her health and her nerves decided for her that it was time for a change. In the public facility, surrounded by all those noisy customers and a large, unruly, disrespectful (in her opinion) staff, she patiently aligned pens by size and in order of color, only to have them moved every single morning when she arrived. It wasn't she who was able to change—it had to be her situation. In her final, joyful position, she was running a one-person doctor's office where all control, arrangement, and appearance depended on her alone. She was the very best employee that doctor ever had.[2]

That's a lot of *why nots* and some pretty frightening scenarios to go along with them. So then *why*, at this point in your life and given all these terrible, worst-case *potential* results, should you even consider beginning on this personal renewal process? What was the worst of the worst you could imagine? "If your answer is not death, complete financial ruin for the rest of my life, or a significant illness—do it! There is nothing to fear. Worst case, you fail and learn something. More likely you will actually not completely fail, and something will come out of it. You just need to start."[3]

Just to be on the safe side, though, it wouldn't hurt to put a few safety nets in place, just for a little extra peace of mind.

Protect Your Job

As was noted earlier, you don't necessarily have to quit tomorrow and go live in a VW van to prove that you're actually renewing your commitment to your values. We all do have bills, we have to eat, and there's that usually immovable roof that needs to be over your head to consider. One answer to this quandary might be "to work towards a new career over time. This might mean making changes in your current job, studying a course in the evening, showing someone in the role or learning new skills. It might also mean that you gradually move into your new career via a series of jobs, rather than one giant leap—and this is important if you want to protect your salary."[4] In other words, *renew*, don't *starve*.

Get Family and Friends Behind You

They just might look at you like you're crazy—at first. But "remember that the fact that your significant other or family member is voicing a few concerns doesn't mean that they think you're a talentless hack who should never chase your dreams. In fact, if you take a moment to step off your high horse and listen, you'll likely discover that the issues they're raising are pretty legitimate and that their intentions are completely pure."[5] Family support during career shifts, changes, or upheavals can provide a lot of the best kinds of input—from an examination of the reality of rent to (potentially) the blind, immeasurable support and confidence that can prompt you to action.

As one now-successful freelance writer once put it, "While I still think that we must reach for our dreams even when naysayers—even if they're our spouses—get in the way, I'm not sure I would have taken such a big leap had my husband not offered . . . emotional and financial support."[6] In other words, you'll go further with someone in your corner.

Preserve Your Sanity

There are no guarantees in life. You might have heard that before. But you picked up this book for a reason and that reason just might be that you're ready to take a few risks for the sake of your sanity. Makes sense. If it's true that you need the support of those closest to you (and it is), then you need your own support—and commitment and belief in yourself—as well, in order to ride out any storms that might be in your way.

Many experts describe what I've been calling values as strengths. As you've read, those are the things we normally think of as what we're good at, but rather they are actually what energize us, make us happy, and that we truly enjoy doing. In order to bolster your own confidence, then, you need to gain strength from your strengths. As you prepare to embark on your renewal, you can support your own peace of mind by knowing that you are following the right dream—yours. The place you'll find yourself in is what author Tom Rath calls "the Strengths Zone,"[7] which sounds like a pretty great place to be. You'll know when you're there when you should no longer:

- Dread going to work
- Have more negative than positive interactions with colleagues
- Treat customers poorly

- Talk about your miserable job
- Fall behind on creativity and achievement[8]

In short, the worst that can happen probably won't happen because your commitment, your family, your friends, and your sanity will be lined up and ready to be your lifeline. When it comes to that, remember what Franklin Roosevelt once said: "When you come to the end of your rope, tie a knot and hang on."[9] Someone else who cares about you will be firmly holding onto the other end.

OK Then, Why?

So, *why* renew? How about this . . . because if "the meaning of life is to find your gift. The purpose of life is to give it away."[10] That truth should be able to convince just about anyone to keep moving forward towards values, contribution, and purpose in their lives.

Having worked through the *who, what, where, and when* of the changes you'd like to start making, we're pausing here, at *why*, just to make sure you are completely comfortable with your intention, the tools, the support, and the reasons for some changes . . . then we can get to *how.* Let's look now at what some of the most important reasons might be.

Because You Have Dreams That Can't Be Ignored

Sometimes our dreams are fuzzy and feature oatmeal or missing a final, but at other times they are clear as glass and simply won't go away. This is one of those times. Still, since we're the only ones who can see them and, obviously, who can feel strongly about making them come true, you just might find yourself answering some questions about your dreams. If anyone wants to know *why* now is dream time for you, here are a few explanations you can offer:

- No one wants to look back with nothing but regret.
- If you don't accomplish something now, you'll likely give up trying—and dreaming.
- By taking action, dreamers become doers. And doers can change the world (at least their corner of it).

- Dreams make you take chances. But chances open up opportunities.
- Even if you fail, you can still take pride in the fact that you tried . . . something new.
- If this dream doesn't work, you can dream another.[11]

So why renew? Maybe it's time your dreams mattered more than what people say about them.

Because You're in the Wrong Job Now, That's for Sure!

Complaining about work has become so clichéd that anyone who really likes their job is often shunned, mocked, or cruelly labeled a Rebecca of Sunnybrook Farm, then ignored. Most often, in social situations especially, anyone who is truly happy with their job isn't likely to admit it for fear of that type of reaction. Low pay, unfair schedules, and mean bosses top the ubiquitous list of complaints, but what does it look like when you really, really hate your job so badly that you'd better get away before it's too late?

- You don't believe in what your organization does, or worse, your principles are challenged by some of its actions. An example of this took place at a library where, under a new director, collections, services, and programs were being heavily censored. Many librarians, committed to the American Library Association's Bill of Rights, saw this shift as something they simply couldn't support. They left.

- You're not being asked to do what you like to do or what you're good at. Lost or underused talents are sneaky things . . . They're bound to find their way to the surface one way—or in one place—or another.

- You can't remember the last time you got to learn something new. Even with technology moving ahead in leaps and bounds in almost every industry (including yours), you are still required to perform twenty-first-century work with twentieth-century equipment and methods.

- You hate it when someone you've just met asks you what you do for a living and you find yourself making something up. The first time you realize that you're so embarrassed by your situation that you don't even want to admit it, the rest of your disappointment will follow like dominoes.

- You're lost all respect for your boss and for most of your colleagues.[12]

Remember, not every person's renewal will require moving to a new job first. "Sometimes, it's not the company that's a bad fit; it's the job responsibilities. [Consider] volunteering for new assignments or projects or taking on new tasks. This may be the spark you need to get through a slump . . . and make things interesting and compelling again."[13] But, okay, if that won't work and changing jobs is what you're going to have to do eventually, that step is not an immovable object around which no other progress can be achieved.

So, why renew? Maybe you just want to quit complaining—and start living.

Because Your Health Is Suffering

"Stress doesn't kill us; we commit suicide with it."[14]

But before we get to that point, unhappiness *at* work and *in* our work can make us sick in lots of creative ways. Ask yourself if you've been experiencing any of these symptoms:

- You've been moody or easily ticked off
- You feel overwhelmed
- You sometimes avoid people
- You have no energy
- Everything hurts—headaches, stomach aches, chest and muscle aches
- You can't sleep
- You are constantly getting colds—one after another[15]

And those are just a few. There are more that are too depressing (or gross) to mention. You're probably not saying *so what,* but just in case you are, consider what experts say all of these aches and pains could lead up to, if you don't turn your life and your stress levels around:

- Real, long-term mental health problems
- Cardiovascular disease
- Eating disorders, including obesity
- Gastro, skin, hair, and other issues that, trust me, you don't want to hear about in great detail[16]

So, why renew? Maybe because "if you don't take care of your body, where do you intend to live?"[17]

Because You Want to Feel Like What You Do Matters

Gone are the days when someone punches a time clock every day for thirty years, changes little other than the inside of a metal lunch box, and then quits due to either ill health or boredom, or both. "It's becoming increasingly important to love your job or industry. As the lines between working life and personal life blur, a job is as much about personal fulfillment and growth as it is about a paycheck. People don't want to make widgets, they want to change lives, including their own."[18]

This reality ties neatly back to the commitment to values discussion that outlines this entire quest. We are more social than we were even fifty years ago. We're more connected and we're more aware of one another's needs. A life of isolation, whether in social or occupational settings, just doesn't cut it anymore for most people.

So, why renew? Just maybe a side effect to your own increased fulfillment could be that you'd be helping someone else along the way.

Because You Want to Keep Learning and Growing

Here's one thing everyone knows for sure. In today's competitive marketplace, "some people will rise to the top. Others will sink to the bottom. Others will stay in the mediocre middle for all of eternity."[19] Why? Usually, it's because they either did or did not grow with their organization, their industry, or within themselves. Maybe you're thinking that, in order to move *your* renewal forward, you're going to have to learn a few new things. Maybe you're right.

When considering into which of the above groups you might fit, consider this: there's a secret to improving your situation, no matter what it is—and it works every single time. "The number one most important tool you absolutely must be utilizing consistently . . . the one thing that will exponentially increase your chances of career success . . . regardless of where you are in your career or where you want to go . . . *you should always be actively participating in professional development and career advancement training.*"[20] If it's beginning to look like training of any kind will be a part of your renewal plan, good for you. There are lots of reasons that learning and growth will pay off:

- Instead of acting like a know-it-all, which no one likes to see, be around, or certainly work for, pursuing professional development demonstrates that you value and seek ongoing knowledge, growth, and skill development.

- Consistency (especially in a boss) is good—rigidity (especially in a boss) is terrible. Be always seeking ongoing training opportunities, to keep fresh, fluid, and open to new ideas.

- Our skills can quickly atrophy, especially with technology changing the tools we use so rapidly. By continually training and stretching our skills, we keep ourselves more open to new challenges—and opportunities.

- Employers want to know that you consider yourself an equal partner in your professional success. And that is something that should be taught in school! Let's repeat it, because it's so important. We need to be equal partners in our own success. If you want to be passed over at best or avoided at worst in your workplace, just go ahead and assume a privileged attitude that lacks all semblance of accountability. With that attitude, your future and your renewal are bound to pass you by.[21]

So, why renew? Hopefully because you realize that learning, growth, and development are investments in your future, and "if you're not willing to invest in yourself, why would anyone else want to?"[22]

Because You Don't Want Work to Feel like a Chore

This one is easy. Because, as has already been stated, the secret to true career happiness is to first find what you love, then to find someone who will pay you to do it.

It must be true, because even Steve Jobs once said, "The only way to do great work is to love what you do. If you haven't found it yet, keep looking. Don't settle."[23] But isn't work supposed to be hard, boring, and unpleasant? Isn't that why they call it work? What right do we have to sit here planning to make things better, more rewarding, and more meaningful every day? Fortunately, it's the twenty-first century now and, finally, we *do* have that right.

One expert offers three steps to undertake in order to make work feel less like, well, work:

- First, change what you do, even by just a little. By being the architect of how you accomplish a task, you just might find the opportunity to learn a new technique or apply a new technology, making the work more fun and more engaging.

- Second, change some relationships at work. That sounds like a great piece of advice I once heard that said, *Don't hang around with dead people.* Spending time with toxic coworkers can drain meaning from even the most meaningful job! Rather, reinvigorate yourself by interacting with positive, valued people.

- Third, don't focus on the parts of your job that you don't like, focus on the parts you do well and of which you can be proud. I once heard of a young woman who was struggling to be successful in college. While all her friends were moving expectantly from one year to the next, she just seemed to be going forward, backward, sideways, but then always forward again. To make ends meet throughout this journey, she worked at a fast food restaurant. While she could have been filled with self-pity, cynicism, frustration, or even shame, she instead took the high road and stayed focused intently on what could be positive about her job. In fact, she once bragged that hers was the cleanest grill in town![24]

The good news is that anyone can take these actions—from any position at work. "You don't have to become a glazier or a zookeeper to find meaning at work. Meaning doesn't take money. At any rank, people can make different meanings of their work and also of themselves at work."[25]

So, why renew? Maybe because while you are where you are, even if your renewal plan will eventually move you forward, you just want to be happier opening that door at work every day.

Because You've Made a Reasoned Decision

There are a lot of decisions you can make when deciding whether or not to make a decision. You can decide to make one, decide to not make one, or decide it's too early to decide because you haven't looked closely enough at the situation. If that's the case, fix it. Get these common challenges[26] out of your way, and, as a former boss once said, "Whether it's a good decision or a bad one, make a damn decision!"[27]

- Make sure you gather all the information you'll need
- Make sure you don't gather too much information, which basically allows you to waste time and put off the decision (and it does nothing but confuse the issue at hand)
- Ask the right people for advice
- Don't ask too many people for advice

So, why renew? Maybe because you just have a feeling that if you put the decision to make some kind of a change aside one more time, it may never come back up again. In other words, there's only one absolute, sure way to miss that brass ring when it comes around . . . by just being too busy to look for it at all.

Because You're Running Out of Time

Back to Steve Jobs, again, who was clearly wise before his time in both life and technology. "Your time is limited, so don't waste it living someone else's life. Don't be trapped by dogma, which is living with the results of other people's thinking. Don't let the noise of others' opinions drown out your own inner voice, heart, and intuition. They somehow already know what you truly want to become. Everything else is secondary."[28]

The key to that comment is . . . your time is limited. It seems that's where the oxymoron often leads us. Either we don't have enough time because life is moving so quickly or we don't have enough time because we're so busy. Either way, as time is the most precious gift we do have, maybe we should spend more of it thinking about spending it well.

Which leads me to the most moving reflection on time I've ever read.

"Don't say you don't have enough time. You have exactly the same number of hours per day that were given to Helen Keller, Pasteur, Michelangelo, Mother Teresa, Leonardo da Vinci, Thomas Jefferson and Albert Einstein."[29]

So, why renew? Maybe just because it's time.

Your Renewal Plan: Step Five—Why?

Looks like there's no shortage of good reasons why you should begin your renewal. Pick one (or more than one) or come up with a reason of your own and complete this next step of your plan. Fill in the lines below, and then recopy your answer onto Line #10 in *Your Renewal Plan* in the back of the book.

I need to stay motivated and remind myself why I'm doing this. Each time I'm tempted to set this goal aside and just go back to *work,* I'm going to remind myself that I *need* and *deserve* this renewal, because . . .

10. _____

Finally, it's time for action. In the next and final chapter of this book, we'll look at *how* to begin your renewal and, within the framework you will build, where to start and how to keep moving forward.

NOTES

1. Joann Dzurenko, conversation, 1997.
2. Lisa Quast, "Overcome the 5 Main Reasons People Resist Change," *Forbes*, November 26, 2012, www.forbes.com/sites/lisaquast/2012/11/26/overcome-the-5-main-reasons-people-resist-change/#54aa7be33393.
3. Pascal Finette, "What's the Worst That Can Happen?" Unreasonable Is, June 19, 2014, http://unreasonable.is/whats-the-worst-that-can-happen/.
4. Charlotte Seager, "Six Tips on How to Make a Successful Career Change," *The Guardian*, October 7, 2014, www.theguardian.com/careers/tips-how-to-make-sucessful-career-change.
5. Kat Boogaard, "How I Convinced My Loved Ones That My Crazy Career Change Wasn't All That Crazy," The Muse, 2016, https://www.themuse.com/advice/how-i-convinced-my-loved-ones-that-my-crazy-career-change-wasnt-all-that-crazy.
6. "Can You Make a Career Change without Family Support?," Heather Sunseri.com, September 9, 2014, http://heathersunseri.com/2014/09/09/can-you-make-a-career-change-without-family-support/.
7. Tom Rath, *Strengths Finder 2.0: A New and Upgraded Edition of the Online Test from Gallup's Now Discover Your Strengths* (New York: Gallup, 2007), 12.
8. Ibid.
9. "When You Reach the End of Your Rope, Tie a Knot in It and Hang On" (quotation), Monticello, 1996, https://www.monticello.org/site/jefferson/when-you-reach-end-your-rope-tie-knot-it-and-hang-quotation.
10. "'The Meaning of Life Is to Find Your Gift, the Purpose of Life Is to Give It Away' - Pablo Picasso," Congruence Framework, May 28, 2015, www.congruenceframework.com/portfolio-items/meaning-life-find-gift-purpose-life-give-away-pablo-picasso/.
11. "19 Reasons to Ignore Everybody and Follow Your Dreams," GloboTreks Travels, "Features," June 21, 2011, www.globotreks.com/features/19-reasons-ignore-everybody-follow-your-dreams/.
12. Stephanie Vozza, "10 Signs You're in the Wrong Job, and What to Do About It," *Fast Company*, October 29, 2014, www.fastcompany.com/3037711/10-signs-youre-in-the-wrong-job-and-what-to-do-about-it.
13. Ibid.

14. Harold J. Williams and Scott Sheperd, *Who's in Charge? Attacking the Stress Myth* (Highland City, FL: Rainbow Books, 1997), 42.

15. "Stress Symptoms: Effects of Stress on the Body," WebMD, July 13, 2015, www.webmd.com/balance/stress-management/stress-symptoms-effects_of -stress-on-the-body?

16. Ibid.

17. Ernie J. Zelinski, *How to Retire Happy, Wild, and Free: Retirement Wisdom That You Won't Get from Your Financial Advisor* (Boreham, Chelmsford, UK: Visions International Publishing, Canada, 2009), 117.

18. Nicole Fallon, *Business News Daily*, May 21, 2015, www.businessnewsdaily .com/7995-reasons-to-do-what-you-love.html.

19. Chrissy Scivicque, "The Most Important Tool for Accelerating Your Career Growth," Eat Your Career, July 1, 2013, www.eatyourcareer.com/2013/07/ the-most-important-tool-for-accelerating-your-career-growth/.

20. Ibid.

21. Ibid.

22. Ibid.

23. Rob Asghar, "Five Reasons to Ignore the Advice to Do What You Love," *Forbes*, April 12, 2013, www.forbes.com/sites/robasghar/2013/04/12/five -reasons-to-ignore-the-advice-to-do-what-you-love/#3b23641a3635.

24. Kirsten Weir, "More Than Job Satisfaction," American Psychological Association, 2016, www.apa.org/monitor/2013/12/job-satisfaction.aspx.

25. Ibid.

26. "Effective Decision Making," Skills You Need, 2011, www.skillsyouneed.com/ ips/decision-making.html.

27. Steve Wood, personal conversation.

28. Marc Chernoff, "10 Lies You Will Hear before You Pursue Your Dreams," Marc and Angel Hack Life, August 30, 2010, www.marcandangel.com/ 2010/08/30/10-lies-you-will-hear-before-you-pursue-your-dreams/.

29. "The Ultimate Guide to Time Management (part 2): Add More Time to Your Day," *Technori*, blog, http://technori.com/2012/10/2615-the-ultimate -guide-to-time-management-part-2-add-more-time-to-your-day/.

HOW DO YOU DO IT?

How we spend our days is, of course, how we spend our lives.

—Annie Dillard

How Do You Eat an Elephant?

The reason most of us stay where we are and just keep hoping for some magic that will make tomorrow better is because that's easier. There's no mystery here. It can be exhausting to examine who you are today and how and why you have made the career and choices you've made along the way. Then, to pause to wonder about what it is you really, really want to be doing, then about when is the right time to do it, and finally about where *in the world* do you start and—bottom line—why bother? Still, you've done all that and made it this far. All that's left now is to take that first step. It's time to figure out what that is.

Any project you take on, any challenge you face, any process you follow, from attending school to cleaning the house, happens one step at a time. What is easy to forget is that first step . . . the one that gets you started.

How do you eat an elephant? Simple. One bite at a time. But, with something that (or this) large in front of you, you better have a plan.

It Wasn't Raining When Noah Built the Ark[1]

Your Renewal Plan has been taking shape throughout your reading of this book. It's got a lot of great foundation in it already. In fact, five of its six steps are done. Finished. Ready. Only two very important parts remain. One is to put some action in it, and lastly, the other is to do it. This chapter will help you with the former. The latter is up to you.

Before adding very real, achievable, and specific steps to complete your plan there are just a few more things you need to do to get every excuse, rationalization, and potential impediment out of your way. Move through these, and then you'll be able to clearly see your future.

First, Do Something about Your Job

Do you love your job or do you hate your job? Or do you live somewhere in between? Have you decided that yet? You've read about the symptoms and the impact of all of these three alternatives, and yet somehow this particular quandary might still hang like an anvil around your neck (or at least a speed bump to your future). Remember, this is not a deal breaker for your renewal, but it is an unhealthy and distracting argument to continually have with yourself. Commit now to do something about it. Maybe not completely resolve it, but to at least put it into perspective and reduce it to a manageable issue (so whatever else is in your life can go on). One more time, consider all your options.

Stay

"Staying in a bad job is both easier and harder than leaving."[2] Still, it can be done, and for lots of reasons, it often should be, at least until better alternatives are developed. What you *never* want to do, though, is quit in place. That's what happens when you decide to stay but do nothing other than impede productivity, exude cynicism, and generally be a pain in the neck. "At work, an ambivalent disposition can be an obstacle. Employers want to see passion. If you don't love your job, you're expected to act as if you do and, every so often, you are called upon to articulate unalloyed enthusiasm."[3] And no, that's not expecting too much, from your employer's perspective. Why? Because negativity in a work team spreads like paper mold in the book sale room. Your bosses don't expect this positivity from you *just* for your benefit . . . it's their job to protect the whole team.

Instead, "use your powers for good instead of evil"[4] and consider making some changes for the better:

- If you were *ever* excited about your job, try to reenergize by finding some new role or activity that can help get that feeling back again.

- See if there's something new going on (or coming down the road) that will affect your job or organization and be the first to learn about it.

- Try warming up your network. That might involve both mending some fences and getting involved and meeting new people. Not only will their positive energy help you stay afloat, but they just might end up being the connections you need when the time does come to move on.[5]

Look

You'll notice this option doesn't read *Go*. That's what might come next, after careful looking. And looking, done right, takes time, patience, and intention. Since no one wants to be in either the frying pan or the fire, it pays, once you've decided it's time to look, to look wisely. Just as the adage advises us to never go to bed mad, neither should we jump from job to job without thoughtful, reasoned, and unemotional purpose.

"Tune in to your intuition before deciding what to do next. If your goals and desires do not come from a secure place within yourself, you will pay undue attention to wet blankets and false friends."[6] At this point, you *have* paid close attention to your values, your purpose, and your future. So that makes you ready to start looking. One more caution, before you leap. Remember what the noted philosopher and humorist Erma Bombeck once demonstrated; the grass isn't always greener, unless you are over the septic tank. Be sure you're leaving for the right reasons and are looking for (and have found) the right solution.

Know "what conflict you are escaping. Dishonesty? Corporate greed? Hypocrisy? Allow yourself to wonder if these qualities are mirrored in your own life—or even in your mind."[7]

With all this clear . . . go ahead and look. But keep your renewal moving forward concurrently, so both your reasons and your solutions can share overlapping success. Maybe the next job you find won't be your perfect job either, but at least you'll be moving closer to where you want to be. "If I lose my direction, I have to look for the North Star, and I go to the north. That does not mean that I expect to arrive at the North Star. I just want to go in that direction."[8] The trick is to just keep moving.

Prepare Yourself for Action

There are plenty of ways to clear the decks and be really ready to get something done. Any student of organizational management will tell you that multiple processes have been used and have changed and evolved over the years, as society has developed and our roles and responsibilities have become clearer.

If you are an observer of the history of the women's movement, for example, you will be amazed at how fragilely and superficially women's interests and focus used to be perceived. Consider these 1949 instructions for undertaking a relatively simple project: sewing.

"Prepare yourself mentally for sewing. Think about what you are going to do. Never approach sewing with a sigh or lackadaisically. Good results are difficult when indifference dominates. Never try to sew with a sink full of dirty dishes or beds unmade. When there are urgent housekeeping chores, do these first so that your mind is free to enjoy your sewing. When you sew, make yourself as attractive as possible. Put on a clean dress. Have your hair in order, powder and lipstick put on. If you are constantly fearful that a visitor might drop in or your husband will come home, and you will not look neatly put together, you will not enjoy your sewing."[9]

Wow. What can this almost 70-year-old example possibly say about preparing to accomplish something today? Maybe that time really, really changes? As you prepare to detail and begin your personal renewal process, there are some more modern-day considerations to keep in mind. For one thing, even with technology, advanced communication, and information overload all around us, it's clear that your focus and mental preparation are critical for project success. However it works for you, get ready, be ready, and stay ready to face successfully the changes that your renewal will undoubtedly bring about. The three steps suggested below might help provide the focus; finding and holding on to the resulting confidence will be up to you.

Find Your Sweet (Work) Spot

If you had the opportunity to work with a professional career counselor, chances are one concept you might be introduced to is developing your career's "sweet spot."[10] For renewal purposes, the elements that make up this special place are just as pertinent and applicable in mid and even end-stage career changes as they are for young professionals just stepping out. That *spot* is the place where three critical concepts intersect and you find yourself doing what you like to do and what you're good at and being paid for it. It may sound easy but, then, so did sewing before all those rules. Minus the restrictions (for the moment, at least) of culture, bias, and competition, you'd be wise to fill in these basics—from the heart—before moving on and committing to specific goals.

Try Being Appreciative

It probably won't be easy or without challenge to move your work and life towards more meaning, so you're going to want to remember to stay positive. Without minimizing the extensive implications of the concept of *appreciative inquiry,* that's very basically what it tells us to do. "Choose a positive focus, identify on times when things are going well, and avoid the natural habit of spotlighting challenges, problems, and tougher times."[11] Later, when your life is more settled again, consider looking further into applying more appreciative habits to everything from leadership to motivation because "in order to carry a positive action, we must develop a positive vision."[12]

Learn Something, Anything New

Both of my first two books were built on the simple concept that if a person could dedicate just one hour each week to their own development, incredible growth could be achieved. This idea was first introduced to me back in the 1980s when I was in library graduate school and our dean pointed out that most people are so busy that they don't take any time out of their schedule to just stop and think. There are lots of reasons offered for a lack of skill development for many professionals, from no time to no money to no purpose. But there is a purpose in learning. No matter where your renewal will lead you, you're undoubtedly going to need to learn something, anything new. "These days, acquiring new professional skills is no longer optional, it's compulsory. The good news is; you don't need a ton of time to learn. The key is; be consistent and focused."[13]

One Bite at a Time

It's time to start on your elephant. A wise person once said, if you don't have a plan written down, you don't have a plan. It's time to finish writing yours, so you can get to work.

In a true, visual sense, strategies begin with big pictures and get narrower from there. You've already done your big-picture work by identifying and committing to your values and, from there, deciding when, where, and why to work them into your life. The final sections of your plan will help you identify specific goals, then prioritize and narrow them down to one on which you can get started. In order to achieve your goal, you'll need to set up a timeline for yourself that outlines the very specific steps that will lead your renewal—and to your success.

Dreaming Big

A high school dance team instructor used to keep her girls focused on great, potential achievements by telling them to "shoot for the moon, and you'll land among the stars."[14] What about you? Given everything you've read and considered so far, it's time to get specific and think about what you'd really, really like to add to your life. Don't think small. Put your action where your values are—shoot for the moon!

"Feeling good about your work, its outcome, and the rewards you receive is a central point to life satisfaction."[15] But having a vision isn't enough; you must transform it into something tangible by setting goals. Here's how you're going to do it.

With all the money and time in the world, we could all probably create a list of hundreds of things we'd love to do. But let's be more realistic. You need to sharpen your focus. Think about what you've been dreaming of, then we'll match it to the work and direction you've uncovered so far. For each of the categories below, enter *just one thing you've always wanted to accomplish* that, every time you've even just *thought* of it, you've felt a surge of adrenaline. What makes you smile, just thinking about it? What would get you out of bed in the morning, excited to begin your day? What would you love to be able to tell everyone that you're doing? In short, what would make you proud, just to know you're involved in it? Fill in something for every category as though the sky's the limit . . . you'll pick a winner to get started on soon enough.

- *Self-Improvement*—Maybe you've always wanted to quilt, or write poetry, or speak another language. There's got to be something you've always thought of doing that, when it pops into your mind, makes you smile? What is it?

  _____

  _____

  _____

- *Relationship Improvement*—When dealing with others, do you feel you come up short? Maybe you're not as great a communicator as you'd like to be? This can involve anything from formal public speaking to making small talk. Or maybe you'd like to be more outgoing? What would make you feel stronger or more comfortable with yourself?

  _____

  _____

  _____

- *Organizational Impact*—Think about all the teams you're involved in, all the groups you have or do work with; everything from the marketing committee at work to your family, church, or neighborhood. Or maybe a larger organizational fit is what you're seeking? Have you always wanted to pursue a leadership position, but just been unconvinced you could succeed? From groups small to large—personal to professional—what have you always wished you could do with other people?

_____

_____

_____

- *The Broader World*—If all politics is truly local, then our communities need us to step up and make a difference. Have there been local, regional, or even broader opportunities for you to be active that you have never pursued? Maybe you've always thought about running for office? The library board? A park board? School board? If everything else in the world was aligned to support this, would you pick one of those or some other opportunity out there in the world? How would you want to make an impact?

_____

_____

_____

- *Professional Influence*—Whether or not you've been a leader in your industry's national, state, or regional organizations, you've probably thought from time to time about something *you* would do, if you had the chance. This could be either to improve the work life or culture for yourself and your colleagues or to make what you all do—as a group—more effective or give it a greater impact. In your mind (at least), remove all the roadblocks that might be in place (pretend you don't have to get more time off work, you don't have to get elected, and you don't have to travel to the far corners of the earth for conferences). How would you like to contribute to improving this industry that matters so much to you?[16]

_____

_____

_____

Parking Lots

You've now listed actions that could lead to improvement in five distinct areas, from improving yourself to relationships, your organization, the world, and your profession. Getting active and involved now in any of these would energize your interests, your passions, and your purpose. All are undoubtedly important to you, but we're not here to change the world overnight. It's time to *park* some of them to come back to later on and to focus on right now on *the one thing* that will truly make you feel renewed. Now it's time to bring together one of your potential goals and one of the accomplishments of which you've dreamed.

Nothing significant has changed. You have no more money or time or influence now than you had back when you used to dream about getting involved and having an impact in one of these areas. The only thing different now is that you've decided—for all the right reasons—to get started.

If, for example, you listed a professional goal as teaching, that doesn't mean you have to quit your job tomorrow and fanatically pursue a PhD so that the local college will hire you. It might, instead, mean you'll take a class on how adults learn. Or you might volunteer to lead a workshop or webinar for your current organization, exploring both the process and the reward you hope to pursue. From those ambitions you just articulated in each of the sections in "Dreaming Big," you're going to select just the *one* to move you forward *right now*. The others can stay safely parked until your next renewal begins.

"Pick something you'd like to share with the world. Think of this project as a present you want to leave behind when you go. Don't worry about it too much. Your first attempts at accomplishing something might be valuable only because they teach you about yourself and how you work. You can't go wrong, if you simply select anything you really love to do."[17]

To keep this critical step aligned with everything you've considered up to this point in the book, go back to Lines # 5, 6, and 7 from *Your Renewal Plan* in the back of the book and rewrite your three "optional" goals below.

5. _____

6. _____

7. _____

Now, pick one.

Pick the one that jumps off the page at you.

Pick the one that makes you feel the most hopeful. Or the one that now, after all you've read and considered about your renewal, holds the greatest promise to make your future your own.

What's Left Is the Moon . . .

An important note to keep you focused on your path: "Most of us generally know what we want in life. For some, it's playing guitar or dancing. For others, it's writing, hiking, spending time with family, photography, or drawing. So, if we know what makes us feel alive, who do we resist it? Why do we avoid doing what we love to do?"[18] Here are just a few common explanations. Whatever else happens, avoid these situations at all costs!

- We fear imperfection. *Just don't.* We all know life is a process, a journey, and a never-ending learning experience. The only mistake we can possibly make that will have any real, negative impact is to stand still and never grow at all.

- Not respecting the process of improvement. It's unlikely that piano virtuosos were born playing the piano or that professional golfers could putt at age two. They grew and improved with time, practice, and a willingness to fail.

As many an innovator will tell you, go ahead and fail, just be sure to fail fast. Then get busy starting again.

- Not accepting your identity. We're not talking about becoming brand-new people here. We're talking about finding a way to incorporate the person who lives deep down inside us into our daily lives in some way—either as part of how we are already making our living or in addition to it. We're creating the story of our life in each moment. You can just think of your renewal as a bit of creative editing.[19]

Your Renewal Plan: Step Six—How? (Part One of Three)

Hopefully, you're ready now to commit to that single goal you selected and get started making this renewal matter for something. With all the fears and excuses out of the way, carefully reread those ideas you just shared for improving yourself, your relationships, your organization, the world, or your profession.

Where does all this intersect and leave you energized to get started? It's there, but don't expect a perfect fit. Rather, think long and hard about where and how you see an overlap that can turn into something that's always been in you—and you're excited about getting it out! This is to be your renewal's specific goal, moving forward. Go ahead and fill it in on the line below:

Here's how it's going to work. Baby steps. Milestones. Small but crucial achievements made one at a time to keep me continually moving forward. I'll be patient but determined and I won't give up on myself. To begin, I need to clearly articulate my goal. It will be to:

11. _____

Now, recopy your answer onto Line #11 in *Your Renewal Plan* in the back of the book. You're on your way, and what's the worst that could happen? You could land among the stars.

A Goal Is a Dream with a Deadline[20]

Congratulations, you have a goal! Now it's time to make it work. But you need some additional encouragement to keep you on track, focused, and committed to see your goal achieved. In short, you need to design a strategy.

"Most people would like to take a more strategic approach to their work, but don't do so because they don't know what doing strategy really means."[21] What it truly means is not as much about *what* you're going to do, but about *how* you're going to do it. So if you're reaching for your calendar, you're on the right track. It's time to set some deadlines.

Remember, though, schedules and date targets won't do you much good if your *life* and other commitments work their way back to the front of your *To Do* list. To keep that from happening, you are going to have to be consistently diligent in managing your time and your energy. A few ideas might help:

- Take a course in something that will help you better manage your own life. Time management courses are outstanding places to start. Take just one and you'll be surprised at how much it can help by giving you back some precious hours or even days of your life.

- Look . . . really look for opportunities to move your goals forward. This technique would be the opposite of thinking: *"If my boss lightens up on me and some time opens up, I'll work on my renewal goals a bit."* Be in charge of your own success.

- Create slack in your life. Following up on the suggestion above, be proactive in looking for ways you can shift your own work in the direction of what really matters to you. In other words, make pursuing your renewal goal *so* important that you consciously make time to achieve it.

- Continually ask yourself *what* you should be doing next. Commit to the *why* and *how* and don't keep going backwards to reinvent that wheel. *What* comes next should be your focus.

- Learn to delegate and organize the rest of your life and work. *"I can't take that class; I mow the lawn on Tuesdays."* Be careful that excuses don't end up becoming part of your eulogy. *"She always wanted to find a way to work in art, and she was very talented, but every time an opportunity came up, she had to mow the lawn."*[22]

Measure Action, Not Minutes

One of the most common mistakes people make when plotting projects is that they make calendar entries for only the deadline. Have you done that? It's your mother-in-law's birthday on April 3, so you dutifully note on your calendar "April 3, Mom's Birthday." Then what happens? You turn the calendar page on April 1 and realize it's too late to send a card now, it will never arrive in two days! Or, at work, you note on your desk blotter (or virtual blotter, or whatever you use) that all personnel evaluations are due to the director on December 1. You'd better not just write that as a *reminder* on December 1. If you're smart, you'll go back and reserve the time needed to complete each and every evaluation long before they're due!

"If you're anything like the typical human . . . there are probably many things—large and small—that you would like to accomplish. That's great, but there is one common mistake we often make when it comes to setting goals . . . The problem is this: set a deadline, but not a schedule."[23] There's a very simple way to overcome that common misstep—and that's to commit to pursuing *this* renewal goal not necessarily by measuring against our performance, but by actions that move us forward.

"Productive and successful people practice the things that are important to them on a consistent basis. The best weightlifters are in the gym at the same time very week. The best writers are sitting down at the keyboard every day. The focus is on doing the action, not on achieving X goal by a certain date."[24]

Take another look at your goal. If you wrote that (as an example) you want to finish that novel, then what you need much more than a deadline (*I'll finish it by December 31, 2017*) is a commitment to make the time to work on it . . . and to not give up. So, you might say *between now and December 31, 2017, I'll find at least 3 hours each week to work on my novel. In fact, I'll commit right now to writing one chapter a month for the next year.* "If you want to be the type of person who accomplishes things [ed., including, most importantly, your own renewal] on a consistent basis, then give yourself a schedule to follow, not a deadline to race towards."[25]

Your Renewal Plan: Step Six—How? (Part Two of Three)

What's your time commitment going to look like? Fill in your plan here, then recopy your answer onto Lines # 12 and 13 in *Your Renewal Plan* in the back of this book.

In order to stay committed to achieving my goal and to really give myself a chance to succeed, I'm going to put on my calendar right now time to work on its progress (when and how often?):

12. _____

With this level of dedication, I'm comfortable that I'll have made significant progress by:

13. _____

This Is Really Happening!

I hate the language of strategic planning. Why? Because it makes the simple act of getting something really important done seem so boring and complicated. Here's an example that brings the process back into perspective:

> She wants to live longer. (That's a goal.)
> She better quit smoking, start exercising, and eat healthier food. (Those are objectives.)

This is when people start rolling their eyes and begin visualizing the shopping list on the refrigerator door. When working with organizations, the trick to establishing great goals is to not just list everything everyone in the room wants to do—but to select goals that fill a real need. And then, to make clear what has to happen back on planet Earth, in the real world, in order for those goals to be achieved.

Objectives can be simple, too. They just clarify what needs to happen before the goal can be achieved or at least what needs to happen to keep you moving forward and in the right direction toward success. "A goal is not always meant to be reached. It often serves simply as something to aim at."[26] So what are you aiming for? And how will you be able to tell whether or not it's a good aim? I would suggest you consider two things:

1. Consider just a few steps to get started, and
2. Be willing to recalculate

"Picture yourself at sea, a hostile ship bearing down on you. You have a limited amount of gunpowder. You take all your gunpowder and use it to fire a big cannonball. The cannonball flies out over the ocean . . . and misses the target, off by 40 degrees. You turn to your stockpile and discover that you're out of gunpowder. You die.

"But, suppose instead that when you see the ship bearing down, you take a little bit of gunpowder and fire a bullet. It misses by 40 degrees. You make another bullet and fire. It misses by 30 degrees. You make a third bullet and fire, missing by only 10 degrees. The next bullet hits—ping!—the hull of the oncoming ship. *Now,* you take all the remaining gunpowder and fire a big cannonball along the same line of sight, which sinks the enemy ship. You live."[27]

Seems sensible, right? So then, instead of putting all your eggs (or gunpowder) in one basket when you begin your renewal, why not just identify a few steps you're fairly sure will get you moving in the right direction, and begin with them? Don't forget that second tip offered earlier, as it is just as critical as the first . . . always be willing to recalculate. In other words, "No matter how far you've gone down the wrong road, turn back."[28] Then start again. Along your journey:

- Remember and reflect often on the *who, what, when, where,* and especially *why* you're doing this in the first place. If you get so discouraged or tripped up that you feel like quitting—reread the earlier chapters of this book.

- Commit your thoughts to paper.[29] There are good reasons this book includes an actual blanks-filled-in copy of Your Renewal Plan. It's no secret. When people write things down, they're much more likely to commit to do them, mainly because:

  › Your memory is a leaking bucket. Even the most well-intentioned ideas and commitments can be easily forgotten as life continues to move along.

  › Ideas, like energy, need to be captured or they could escape or be kidnapped.

  › Writing a plan down brings it into focus and it can act as a powerful and successful life raft in changing waters.

  › You'll feel calmer, more relaxed, and much less stressed when you realize you don't have to remember everything about a project . . . your plan will remember it for you! And less stress almost always equals more success![30]

Your Renewal Plan: Step Six—How? (Part Three of Three)

Okay, it's time to write and wrap this plan up. Coming down from the lofty world of goals, it's time to think of those first steps toward realizing one of your lifelong dreams. That makes it sound worthwhile, right? This is the exciting part. This is where you get to decide how and what comes next.

Will you be taking classes? Looking for a new job? Expanding your current job? Mentoring someone? What? You should begin with the same process used previously in this book. Rewrite your goal from Line 11 below and then, under it, write at least ten things, actions, or steps that would help you achieve it. Don't stop early . . . write at least ten . . . and write even more if you can think of them.

In Order to Reach My Goal of:

_____

Several Things Need to Happen/Take Place, in no particular order:

1. _____

2. _____

3. _____

4. _____

5. _____

6. _____

7. _____

8. _____

9. _____

10. _____

At this point, you might just be expecting to hear that, of all of those ten actions you listed, you need to put them in order of complexity or cost or impact—but that's not going to be suggested at all.

Instead, *rate* each of the ten, on a 1–10 scale, according to these criteria:

10—OMG! I can't wait to start this one.
9—I've always wanted to try this.
8—This one is going to be *fun!*

All the way down to:

2—Yeah, okay, I want to try this, too!

And

1—I can do this . . . I *know* I can!

You get the picture. Then, of course, rewrite, reword, schmooze out, or otherwise clearly articulate your *top three*, and enter them below:

It's time to stop thinking about it—and to get started. In order to reach my goal successfully, I'll start by working on these three things:

14. _____

15. _____

16. _____

Next, recopy these answers onto Lines #14, 15, and 16 in *Your Renewal Plan* in the back of this book.

NOW, You Have a Plan

"Rest when you're weary. Refresh and renew yourself, your body, your mind, your spirit. Then get back to work."[31]

Good advice. It's time now for you to get back to work, but hopefully you'll be going back a bit more energized and focused than you were when you picked up this book. Hopefully, *Your Renewal Plan* will go back to work with you and, together, you'll keep an excitement for work alive. But you're going to have to return the favor. Don't stop tweaking, polishing, and renewing your plan and your goals until and unless they are *fun, exciting and really, really challenging.*

Because that's what true renewal looks like.

Otherwise, we're just working.

To close, here's a thought for all of us who have great ideas, like renewing ourselves, but then lose steam at the thought of tilting at such an enormous windmill. How can we do it, really? How can we possibly succeed at such an enormous task?

"Actually, I just woke up one day and decided I didn't want to feel like that anymore, or ever again. So I changed. Just like that."[32]

NOTES

1. "Double-Tongued Word Wrester Dictionary," Barry Popik, 2008, www .barrypopik.com/index.php/new_york_city/entry/it_wasnt_raining_when _noah_built_the_ark.
2. Christie Mims, "4 Ways to Know It's Time to Quit Your Job," World Economic Forum, 2016, https://www.weforum.org/agenda/2015/04/4-ways-to-know -its-time-to-quit-your-job/.
3. Tracy Moore, "No, You Absolutely Do Not Have to Love Your Job," Jezebel, February 17, 2015, http://jezebel.com/no-you-absolutely-do-not-have-to -love-your-job-1686132756.
4. Dianne Discenzo, personal conversation.
5. Mims, "4 Ways to Know"
6. Cathy Goodwin, "Ten Things to Do If You Really, Really Hate Your Job," Experience by Simplicity, 2016, https://www.experience.com/alumnus/

article?channel_id=career_management&source_page=additional_articles
&article_id=article_1170473321734.

7. Ibid.

8. "Living Life Fully," www.livinglifefully.com/journey.html.

9. David Mikkelson, "Advice from a 1949 Singer Sewing Manual," Snopes, January 23, 2015, www.snopes.com/history/document/sewing.asp.

10. Janet Wall, "Finding the Sweet Spot for Career Success," *The Career Development Quarterly* (Spring 2016): 16–18.

11. Donald A. Schutt, *A Strength-Based Approach to Career Development Using Appreciative Inquiry* (Broken Arrow, OK: National Career Development Association, 2007), 12.

12. "'In Order to Carry a Positive Action We Must Develop Here a Positive Vision,' Dalai Lama," iamraok—Random Acts of Kindness—Wordpress, September 5, 2013, https://iamraok.wordpress.com/2013/09/05/in-order-to -carry-a-positive-action-we-must-develop-here-a-positive-vision-dalai-lama/.

13. Nicole Cavazos, "How to Learn a New Job Skill in Just 15 Minutes a Day," ZipRecruiter.com, "Job Search Tips," January 27, 2015, https://www.zip recruiter.com/blog/learn-new-job-skills-15-minutes-a-day/.

14. Kathy Werner, personal conversation.

15. Caitlin Williams and Annabelle Reitman, *Career Moves: Be Strategic about Your Future* (Alexandria, VA: American Society for Training and Development, 2012), 108.

16. "Creating Personal Leadership Plans: My Leadership Development Plan," What Are Good Leadership Skills, www.what-are-good-leadership-skills .com/personal-leadership.

17. Barbara Sher, *What Should I Do When I Want to Do Everything? Refuse to Choose! A Revolutionary Program for Doing All That You Love* (Emmaus, PA: Rodale Books, 2006), 249.

18. "Why Do We Avoid Doing What We Love?" Pick the Brain, Motivation and Self Improvement, June 12, 2008, www.pickthebrain.com/blog/why-do-we -avoid-doing-what-we-love/.

19. Ibid.

20. "A Goal Is a Dream with a Deadline," Lingholic, "Goals," April 2, 2013, www .lingholic.com/a-goal-is-a-dream-with-a-deadline/.

21. Herminia Ibarra, "Six Ways to Grow Your Job," *Harvard Business Review*, "Career Planning," September 25, 2013, https://hbr.org/2013/09/six-ways -to-grow-your-job/.

22. Ibid.

23. James Clear, "How to Achieve Your Goals (This Simple Trick Makes Progress Easy)," James Clear, "Goal Setting," February 21, 2013, http://jamesclear.com/ schedule-goals.

24. Ibid.

25. Ibid.

26. "'A Goal Is Not Always Meant to Be Reached, It Often Serves Simply as Something to Aim at,'" Lifehacker, January 21, 2013, http://lifehacker.com/5977645/a-goal-is-not-always-meant-to-be-reached-it-often-serves-simply-as-something-to-aim-at.

27. Jim Collins and Morten T. Hansen, *Great by Choice: Uncertainty, Chaos, and Luck: Why Some Thrive Despite Them All* (New York: HarperCollins, 2011), 78–79.

28. John D. Krumboltz and Al S. Levin, *Luck Is No Accident: Making the Most of Happenstance in Your Life and Career* (Atascadero, CA: Impact, 2008), 75.

29. Williams, *Career Moves.*

30. Henrik Edberg, "7 Powerful Reasons Why You Should Write Things Down," *The Positivity Blog*, www.positivityblog.com/index.php/2010/09/30/write-things-down/.

31. "Ralph Marston Quotes at BrainyQuote.Com," BrainyQuote, 2001, www.brainyquote.com/quotes/quotes/r/ralphmarst132647.html.

32. "Motivational," Pinterest, https://www.pinterest.com/pin/190980840418761241/.

MY RENEWAL PLAN

Step 1

From "Who," pp. 1–8

The three things I most deeply value are:

1. _____
2. _____
3. _____

Step 2

From "What," pp. 19–33

Now that I see what really matters to me and where my strengths can help me make a difference, I'm going to find a way to get involved in the area of:

4. _____

I can think of several ways I can do this but, to get the ball rolling, I'm going to seriously consider these three options and then, later, I'll focus in on just one when it's time to set my first goal:

5. _____
6. _____
7. _____

Step 3

From "When," pp. 35–49

It's time to do something *I* want to do. Keeping in mind the distractions (which I'll manage), challenges (which I'll respect but keep in perspective), or procrastination (which I will train myself to overcome), I'm going to remember that *this* is the right time to make a change because:

8. _____

_____

Step 4

From "Where," pp. 51–69

Where I am right now is the perfect place from which to launch by renewal, because whether I decide to stay or go, all things considered,

9. _____

_____

Step 5

From "Why," pp. 71–86

I need to stay motivated and remind myself why I'm doing this. Each time I'm tempted to set this goal aside and just go back to *work*, I'm going to remind myself that I *need* and *deserve* this renewal, because . . .

10. _____

_____

Step 6 (3 Parts)

From "How," pp. 87–106

Here's how it's going to work. Baby steps. Milestones. Small but crucial achievements made one at a time to keep me continually moving forward. I'll be patient but determined and I won't give up on myself. To begin, I need to clearly articulate one single (for now) goal. It will be to:

11. _____

In order to stay committed to achieving my goal and to really give myself a real chance to succeed, I'm going to put on my calendar right now time to work on its progress (when and how often?):

12. _____

With this level of dedication, I'm comfortable that I'll have made significant progress by:

13. _____

It's time to stop thinking about it—and to get started. In order to reach my goal successfully, I'll start by working on these three things:

14. _____

15. _____

16. _____

Congratulations, now you have a plan!

BIBLIOGRAPHY

Ahang, Maggie. "Here's Why So Many People Hate Their Jobs." Business Insider. http://1.http://www.businessinsider.com/reasons-you-hate-your-job-2014-6.

Asghar, Rob. "Five Reasons to Ignore the Advice to Do What You Love." *Forbes*. April 12, 2013. www.forbes.com/sites/robasghar/2013/04/12/five-reasons-to-ignore-the-advice-to-do-what-you-love/#3b23641a3635.

Bedard, Paul. "Rudolph's Pal 'Hermey the Elf' Gets His Dentist's Degree after 50 Years." *The Washington Examiner*. November 20, 2014. www.washingtonexaminer.com/rudolphs-pal-hermey-the-elf-gets-his-dentists-degree-after-50-years/article/2556397.

Biro, Meghan M. "How to Make Work Matter." *Forbes*. March 9, 2014. http://1.http://www.forbes.com/sites/meghanbiro/2014/03/09/how-to-make-work-matter/#46b4e4811ba9.

Bolles, Richard N. *How to Find Your Mission in Life*. Berkeley, CA: Ten Speed, 2000.

Boogaard, Kat. "How I Convinced My Loved Ones That My Crazy Career Change Wasn't All That Crazy." The Muse. 2016. https://www.themuse.com/advice/how-i-convinced-my-loved-ones-that-my-crazy-career-change-wasnt-all-that-crazy.

BrainyQuote. "Eddie Cantor Quotes at BrainyQuote.Com." 2001. www.brainyquote.com/quotes/quotes/e/eddiecant0309843.html.

Brett, Regina. *God Is Always Hiring: 50 Lessons for Finding Fulfilling Work*. New York: Grand Central Publishing, Hachette Book Group, 2015.

Brown, Jackson H. "A Quote by H. Jackson Brown Jr." Goodreads. May 29, 2016. www.goodreads.com/quotes/7992-don-t-say-you-don-t-have-enough-time-you-have-exactly.

Buckingham, Marcus. "Know Your Strengths, Own Your Strengths." Leanin. http://leanin.org/education/know-your-strengths-own-your -strengths-no-one-else-will/.

Caldwell, Allison Shaw. May 2, 2016. https://www.facebook.com.

Cardy, Alison Elissa. "The 2 Biggest Reasons You Can't Decide on a Career Direction." *Brazen.com*. November 1, 2012. http://1.http:// www.brazen.com/blog/archive/career-growth/the-2-biggest-reasons -you-cant-decide-on-a-career-direction/.

"Career Planning: Should Your Student Work Part-Time During College?" UniversityParent. http://1.https://www.universityparent .com/topics/career-planning/should-your-student-work-part-time -during-college-2/#gsc.tab=0.

Cavazos, Nicole. "How to Learn a New Job Skill in Just 15 Minutes a Day." ZipRecruiter.com. "Job Search Tips." January 27, 2015. https://www.ziprecruiter.com/blog/learn-new-job-skills-15-minutes -a-day/.

Chernoff, Marc. "10 Lies You Will Hear before You Pursue Your Dreams." Marc and Angel Hack Life. August 30, 2010. www.marc andangel.com/2010/08/30/10-lies-you-will-hear-before-you-pursue -your-dreams/.

Choi, Janet. "Why Does Your Work Matter?" *idonethis* blog. August 2014. http://blog.idonethis.com/why-does-your-work-matter/.

Clear, James. "How to Achieve Your Goals (This Simple Trick Makes Progress Easy)." James Clear. "Goal Setting." February 21, 2013. http://jamesclear.com/schedule-goals.

Collins, Jim, and Morten T. Hansen. *Great by Choice: Uncertainty, Chaos, and Luck: Why Some Thrive Despite Them All.* New York: HarperCollins, 2011.

Confucius. "Quote Investigator." September 2, 2014. http://quoteinvesti gator.com/2014/09/02/job-love/.

Constable, Kimanzi. "5 Signs You're Not Happy with Your Life (and What You Can Do About It)." HuffingtonPost.com. October 2, 2015. www.huffingtonpost.com/kimanzi-constable/5-signs-youre -not-happy-with-your-life-and-what-you-can-do-about-it_b_ 8166980.html.

"Creating Personal Leadership Plans: My Leadership Development Plan." What Are Good Leadership Skills. www.what-are-good -leadership-skills.com/personal-leadership.

Cushing, Richard. "20 Quotes: The Importance of Planning." BCG Consulting—Ormond Rankin. June 15, 2012. https://ormondrankin .wordpress.com/2012/06/15/20-quotes-the-importance-of-planning/.

"Dear Abby." No date available; personal recollection.

Delaney, Chad. Refreshing the World. Mantua, OH: Mantua Center Christian Church, 2016.

DeMers, Jayson. "7 Reasons You Hate Your Job." Inc.com. October 29, 2014. www.inc.com/jayson-demers/7-reasons-you-hate-your-job .html.

Dillard, Annie. "A Quote from the Writing Life." Goodreads. 2016. www.goodreads.com/quotes/1204-how-we-spend-our-days-is-of -course-how-we.

"Do You Know Your Skill Set?" AARP Foundation. Worksearch In- formation Network. www.aarpworksearch.org/RESEARCH/Pages/ JobsinDemand.aspx.

Economy, Peter. "Want to Be Successful and Happy? Don't Make These 5 Deadly Career Mistakes." January 23, 2016. www.inc.com/peter -economy/5-career-mistakes-you-should-never-make.html.

Edberg, Henrik. "Gandhi's 10 Rules for Changing the World." Daily Good. 2013. www.dailygood.org/story/466/gandhi-s-10-rules-for -changing-the-world-henrik-edberg/.

———. "101 Inspiring Happiness Quotes." The Positivity Blog. "Con- fucius." www.positivityblog.com/index.php/2013/08/20/happiness -quotes/.

———. "7 Powerful Reasons Why You Should Write Things down." The Positivity Blog. www.positivityblog.com/index.php/2010/09/30/ write-things-down/.

"Effective Decision Making." Skills You Need. 2011. www.skillsyou need.com/ips/decision-making.html.

Eikenberg, Darcy. "To Stay or Leave Your Job? Four Secrets to Help You Decide." Red Cape Revolution. January 31, 2013. http://redcape revolution.com/secrets-to-stay-or-leave-your-job/.

Fallon, Nicole. Business News Daily. May 21, 2015. www.businessnews daily.com/7995-reasons-to-do-what-you-love.html.

Finette, Pascal. "What's the Worst That Can Happen?" Unreasonable Is. June 19, 2014. http://unreasonable.is/whats-the-worst-that-can -happen/.

Forum, Forbes Leadership. "How to Make Big Career Decisions: Don't Tack to Cover." *Forbes*. July 19, 2011. www.forbes.com/sites/ forbesleadershipforum/2011/07/19/how-to-make-big-career-decisions -dont-tack-to-cover/#1373d95c5597.

Gallo, Amy. "Don't Like Your Job? Change It (without Quitting)." *Harvard Business Review*. June 19, 2012. https://hbr.org/2012/06/dont-like -your-job-change-it-w/.

Garnett, Laura. "Five Signs That You're Maximizing Your Potential." Inc.com. June 2016. www.inc.com/laura-garnett/5-signs-that-youre -maximizing-your-potential.html.

Givertz, Amitai. "Should I Stay or Should I Go? 7 Arguments For and Against Leaving Your Job." Salary.com. www.salary.com/should-i -stay-or-should-i-go-7-arguments-for-and-against-leaving-your-job/.

Goodwin, Cathy. "Ten Things to Do If You Really, Really Hate Your Job." Experience by Simplicity. 2016. https://www.experience .com/alumnus/article?channel_id=career_management&source_ page=additional_articles&article_id=article_1170473321734.

Grant, Adam. "The One Question You Should Ask about Every New Job." Sunday Review, *New York Times*. March 28, 2016. www.nytimes .com/2015/12/20/opinion/sunday/the-one-question-you-should-ask -about-every-new-job.html?_r=0.

Grodin, Charles. *If I Only Knew Then . . . : Learning from Our Mistakes.* New York: Springboard, 2007.

Hakala, Werner M. "Night, Montreal." Personal copy of poem, n.p. Ashtabula, Ohio. n.d.

Hakala-Ausperk, Catherine. *Be a Great Boss: One Year to Success.* Chicago: American Library Association, 2011.

Hamm, Trent. "About." The Simple Dollar. 2016. www.thesimpledollar .com/about/.

———. "Downgrading Your Job, Not Your Life." The Simple Dollar. March 1, 2011. www.thesimpledollar.com/downgrading-your-job-without -downgrading-your-life/.

"Healing Hugs." Facebook. http://https://www.facebook.com/healinhugs/
photos/a.76195251739.74070.75851286739/10154093848151740/?
type=3&theater.

Hill, Napoleon. "Goal Quotes at BrainyQuote." BrainyQuote. 2001.
www.brainyquote.com/quotes/keywords/goal.html.

HubPages. "Motivational." Pinterest. https://www.pinterest.com/
pin/190980840418761241/.

Hyatt, Michael, and Daniel Harkavy. *Living Forward: A Proven Plan to
Stop Drifting and Get the Life You Want.* Ada, MI: Baker Academ-
ic, division of Baker Publishing Group, 2016.

Ibarra, Herminia. "Six Ways to Grow Your Job." *Harvard Business Review*.
"Career Planning." September 25, 2013. https://hbr.org/2013/09/
six-ways-to-grow-your-job/.

Johnson, Shana Montesol. "Do Not Make a Career Decision without
This List." Development Crossroads. http://developmentcrossroads
.com/2011/08/career-decision-list/.

Jones, Laurie Beth. "Inspiring Personal Growth: What Is Your USP?"
Jones Group, in e-mail blog, June 11, 2015.

Jones, Patrick. Conversation. 1989.

Kaye, Beverly, and Julie Winkle Giulioni. *Help Them Grow or Watch
Them Go: Career Conversations Employees Want.* San Francisco:
Berrett-Koehler, 2012.

Kirby, Michael. "Since Childhood He Knew He Wanted to Help Others."
AuburnJournal.com. September 19, 2008. http://1.http://www.auburn
journal.com/article/childhood-he-knew-he-wanted help others.

Kjerulf, Alexander. "5 Signs Your Body Wants You to Quit Your Job."
Care2. 2016. www.care2.com/greenliving/how-your-job-makes-you
-sick.html.

Klosowski, Thorin. "Why It's Worth Job Hopping in Your 20s." Lifehacker.
November 5, 2014. http://lifehacker.com/why-its-worth-job-hopping
-in-your-20s-1655008192.

"KNOW YOURSELF Quotes Like Success." Like Success. 2015. http://
likesuccess.com/topics/18209/know-yourself/2.

Krumboltz, John D., and Al S. Levin. *Luck Is No Accident: Making the
Most of Happenstance in Your Life and Career.* Atascadero, CA: Impact, 2008.

Lama, Dalai. "Positive Quotes at BrainyQuote." BrainyQuote. 2001. www.brainyquote.com/quotes/topics/topic_positive.html.

Latumahina, Donald. "Achieving Your Dream: How to Take the First Step." Lifehack.org. http://1.http://www.lifehack.org/articles/pro ductivity/achieving-your-dream-how-to-take-the-first-step.html.

Lawrence. "Making a Big Life Change Is Pretty Scary. But Know What's Even Scarier? Regret." Tofurious Marketing Strategies for Smart Creatives. August 3, 2012. http://tofurious.com/quotes/making-a-big -life-change-is-pretty-scary-but-know-whats-even-scarier-regret/.

"Learn to Recognise Your True Strengths—Hint: They Aren't Just What You're Good At." Ignite Global, 1. http://igniteglobal.com/learn-to -recognise-your-true-strengths-hint-they-arent-just-what-you-are -good-at/.

Lee, Bruce. "Goal Quotes at BrainyQuote." BrainyQuotes. 2001. www .brainyquote.com/quotes/keywords/goal.html.

Marks, Shala. "4 Negative Effects of a Disorganized Company." Recruiter .com. August 12, 2013. https://www.recruiter.com/i/4-negative-effects -of-a-disorganized-company/.

Marston, Ralph. "Ralph Marston Quotes at BrainyQuote.Com." BrainyQuotes. 2001. www.brainyquote.com/quotes/quotes/r/ralph marst132647.html.

McFarlin, Kate. "Importance of Relationships in the Workplace." *Small Business Chron*. 2016. http://smallbusiness.chron.com/importance -relationships-workplace-10380.html.

Mead, Jonathan. "Why Do We Avoid Doing What We Love?" Pick the Brain, Motivation and Self Improvement. June 12, 2008. www .pickthebrain.com/blog/why-do-we-avoid-doing-what-we-love/.

Mikkelson, David. "Advice from a 1949 Singer Sewing Manual." Snopes. January 23, 2015. www.snopes.com/history/document/sewing.asp.

Miller, John G. *QBQ! The Question Behind the Question: What to Really Ask Yourself: Practicing Personal Accountability in Business and in Life*. Denver, CO: Putnam, 2004.

Mims, Christie. "4 Ways to Know It's Time to Quit Your Job." World Economic Forum. 2016. https://www.weforum.org/agenda/2015/04/ 4-ways-to-know-its-time-to-quit-your-job/.

Moore, Tracy. "No, You Absolutely Do Not Have to Love Your Job." Jezebel. February 17, 2015. http://jezebel.com/no-you-absolutely-do-not-have-to-love-your-job-1686132756.

Mulvey, Jeanette. "Parents May Have Big Impact on Career Choices." LiveScience. December 3, 2010. http://1.http://www.livescience.com/9059-parents-big-impact-career-choices.html.

"9 Career Change Success Stories That Will Seriously Inspire You." The Muse. http://1.https://www.themuse.com/advice/why-i-quit-my-job-and-rowed-across-3-oceans.

Norbert. "19 Reasons to Ignore Everybody and Follow Your Dreams." GloboTreks Travels. June 21, 2011. www.globotreks.com/features/19-reasons-ignore-everybody-follow-your-dreams/.

Perna, Laura W. "Understanding the Working College Student." AAUP.org. May 3, 2013. http://1.http://www.aaup.org/article/understanding-working-college-student#.Vy08aBUrKCQ.

Picasso, Pablo. "The Meaning of Life Is to Find Your Gift. The Purpose of Life Is to Give It." https://quotefancy.com/quote/34224/Pablo-Picasso-The-meaning-of-life-is-to-find-your-gift-The-purpose-of-life-is-to-give-it.

"Popular Gambling and Betting Quotes and Sayings." Lootmeister.com. www.lootmeister.com/betting/quotes.php.

Posner, Roy. "A New Way of Living: Essays on Human Evolution and Transformation." Aurobindo.ru. 2010. http://1.http://www.aurobindo.ru/workings/other/roy_posner-a_new_way_of_living.pdf.

Quast, Lisa. "Overcome the 5 Main Reasons People Resist Change." *Forbes*. November 26, 2012. www.forbes.com/sites/lisaquast/2012/11/26/overcome-the-5-main-reasons-people-resist-change/#54aa7bc33393.

Quoteland. "Life Quotes: Quoteland: Quotations by Topic." 1997. www.quoteland.com/topic/Life-Quotes/95/.

Rath, Tom. *Strengths Finder 2.0: A New and Upgraded Edition of the Online Test from Gallup's Now Discover Your Strengths*. New York: Gallup, 2007.

Roosevelt, Franklin D. "Quotes about Sanity (307 Quotes)." Goodreads. 2016. www.goodreads.com/quotes/tag/sanity.

Roosevelt, Theodore. "Decision Quotes." BrainyQuote. www.brainyquote.com/quotes/keywords/decision.html.

Schutt, Donald A. *A Strength-Based Approach to Career Development Using Appreciative Inquiry.* Broken Arrow, OK: National Career Development Association, 2007.

Scivicque, Chrissy. "The Most Important Tool for Accelerating Your Career Growth." Eat Your Career. July 1, 2013. www.eatyourcareer .com/2013/07/the-most-important-tool-for-accelerating-your-career -growth/.

Seager, Charlotte. "Six Tips on How to Make a Successful Career Change." *The Guardian.* October 7, 2014. www.theguardian.com/ careers/tips-how-to-make-sucessful-career-change.

Serf-Walls, Lamisha. "7 Signs You're Ready for a Major Life Change." HuffingtonPost.com. May 9, 2015. http://1.http://www.huffington post.com/lamisha-serfwalls/7-signs-youre-ready-for-a-major-life -change_b_7225108.html.

"7 Key Questions: Who, What, Why, When, Where, How, How Much?—Consultant's Mind." Consultant's Mind. July 24, 2015. www .consultantsmind.com/2015/07/24/7-key-questions/.

Sher, Barbara. *I Could Do Anything If I Only Knew What It Was.* New York: Dell, 1994.

———. *What Should I Do When I Want to Do Everything? Refuse to Choose! A Revolutionary Program for Doing All That You Love.* Emmaus, PA: Rodale Books, 2006.

Sher, Barbara, and Annie Gottlieb. *BT-Wishcraft.* New York: Ballantine Books, 1983.

"Simple Definition of Renewal." Merriam-Webster. http://1.http://www .merriam-webster.com/dictionary/renewal.

Smith, Jacquelyn. "14 Signs It's Time to Leave Your Job." *Forbes.* September 4, 2013. www.forbes.com/sites/jacquelynsmith/2013/09/04/14 -signs-its-time-to-leave-your-job/#4691a28e706f.

"Stress Symptoms: Effects of Stress on the Body." WebMD. July 13, 2015. www.webmd.com/balance/stress-management/stress-symptoms -effects_of-stress-on-the-body?

Sunseri, Heather. "Can You Make a Career Change without Family Support?" Heather Sunseri.com. September 9, 2014. http://heather sunseri.com/2014/09/09/can-you-make-a-career-change-without -family-support/.

"10 Secrets to a Successful Retirement." Next Avenue. August 13, 2012. www.nextavenue.org/10-secrets-successful-retirement/.

Tescia. "21 Best Part-Time Jobs for Teens and High School Students— Localwise." Localwise, *Get a Job!* January 30, 2016. https://www.local wisejobs.com/blog/21-best-part-time-jobs-for-teens-and-high -school-students/.

"The Best Guide to Life: Your Personal Values." Wisconsin Relation- ship Education. http://wire.wisc.edu/yourself/selfreflectknowyour self/Yourpersonalvalues.aspx.

"There's No Such Thing as the Wrong Decision." KateNorthrup.com. February 24, 2016. http://katenorthrup.com/theres-no-such-thing-as -the-wrong-decision/.

Thompson, Scott. "The Importance of Non-Financial Rewards for the Organization." *Small Business Chron,* 2016. http://smallbusiness.chron .com/importance-nonfinancial-rewards-organization-45146.html.

Vozza, Stephanie. "10 Signs You're in the Wrong Job, and What to Do about It." *Fast Company.* October 29, 2014. www.fastcompany .com/3037711/10-signs-youre-in-the-wrong-job-and-what-to-do -about-it.

Walker, Rose. "The Audacity of HOPE (for Job Seekers)." May 4, 2016. https://www.linkedin.com/pulse/audacity-hope-job-seekers-rose -walker?trk=mp-reader-card.

Wall, Janet. "Finding the Sweet Spot for Career Success." *Career Devel- opment Quarterly* (Spring 2016): 16.

Warhol, Andy. "Changes Quotes at BrainyQuote." BrainyQuote. 2001. www.brainyquote.com/quotes/keywords/changes.html.

Weir, Kirsten. "More Than Job Satisfaction." American Psychological Association. 2016. www.apa.org/monitor/2013/12/job-satisfaction .aspx.

Wert, Ken. "7 Tips for Making Happy Decisions about How to Spend Your Time, Energy, and Money." Gretchen Rubin. "Efficiency." July 13, 2011. http://gretchenrubin.com/happiness_project/2011/07/7 -tips-for-making-happy-decisions-about-how-to-spend-your-time -energy-and-money/.

White, John. "I Thought My Career Was Over Until I Did These 5 Things." Inc.com. June 2, 2016. www.inc.com/john-white/5-power-tips-to -rescue-your-career-from-the-brink-of-failure.html.

White, William J. "From Day One: CEO Advice to Launch an Extraordinary Career." Pearson: Higher Education. 2006. https://www.pearsonhighered.com/samplechapter/0132206862.pdf.

"Why Good Employees Leave? David W Richard." TheLayoff.com. December 15, 2013. https://www.thelayoff.com/t/tbnQdtP.

Wikipedia. s.v. "Five Ws." 2016. https://en.wikipedia.org/wiki/Five_Ws.

———. s.v. "I know it when I see it." 2016. https://en.wikipedia.org/wiki/I_know_it_when_I_see_it.

———. s.v. "Japanese proverbs." 2016. https://en.wikipedia.org/wiki/Japanese_proverbs.

———. s.v. "Maslow's hierarchy of needs." 2016. https://en.wikipedia.org/wiki/Maslow%27s_hierarchy_of_needs.

———. s.v. "Synanon." 2016. https://en.wikipedia.org/wiki/Synanon. Attributed to Charles E. Dederich, Sr.

Williams, Caitlin, and Annabelle Reitman. *Career Moves: Be Strategic about Your Future.* Alexandria, VA: American Society for Training and Development, 2012.

Williams, Harold J., and Scott Sheperd. *Who's in Charge? Attacking the Stress Myth.* Highland City, FL: Rainbow Books, 1997.

Williams, Ray. "Are We Hardwired to Be Positive or Negative?" PsychologyToday.com. 1991. https://www.psychologytoday.com/blog/wired-success/201406/are-we-hardwired-be-positive-or-negative.

"Work Values—What Do You Find Really Important in Your Job?" 123Test. 2016. https://www.123test.com/work-values/.

Zelinski, Ernie J. *How to Retire Happy, Wild, and Free: Retirement Wisdom That You Won't Get from Your Financial Advisor.* Boreham, Chelmsford, UK: Visions International, Canada, 2009.

Zupek, Rachel. "Can Birth Order Determine Your Career?" October 2008. http://1.http://www.cnn.com/2008/LIVING/worklife/10/22/cb.birth.order.career/index.html?iref=24hours.

INDEX

change (*cont.*)
    plateauing as sign of need for,
        44–45
    in work habits, 82
    worries about, 72–77
clarity, 66
Coffman, Curt, 55
colleagues, 61
community involvement, 93–94
confidence, 66
Confucius, 51, 66
control
    fear of losing, 73–74
    for selection of next job, 66
culture
    work/life balance and, 63
    of workplace, 53

D

deadline
    goal as dream with, 97–98
    schedule vs., 98–99
Dear Abby, 35
decision making
    about staying/leaving current job,
        51–52
    quitting job, final steps before,
        64–65
    reasoned decision for renewal, 83
    reasons for staying or leaving
        current job, 52–64
    selection of next job, 66
    timing of, 35–36
    worries about change, 72–77
Dederich, Charles E. "Chuck," Sr., 35
Delaney, Chad, 19
Dillard, Annie, 87
direction, xiv
Downgrade Your Job, Not Your Life
    (Hamm), 65–66
dreams
    dreaming big, 92–94
    goal as dream with deadline, 97–98

as reason for renewal, 77–78
strengths for following, 76–77
in teenage years, 40
things that you have always wanted
    to do, 8–9
what you would love to do, 25–28

E

easiness, 25–26
Economy, Peter, 14–15
employment
    See job; work
energy
    consideration of what energizes
        you, 28–30
    for work, 27
ethics, 53
exercises
    life cycle of purpose, 46–47
    life so far, review of, 8–10
    list of what you did, 22–24
    list of what you do now, 24–25
    reasons to finish this book list, 17
    values, top twenty, 5–7
    Who Are You?, 17
    See also Renewal Plan

F

Facebook, xviii
family
    support of, 75–76
    work/life balance and, 62–64
fear
    of change, reasons for, 72–77
    of decisions, 35–36
    of imperfection, 96
    of unknown, 72
Fey, Tina, 43
5W1H, xvii–xx
focus
    goals, list of, 92–94
    as preparation for action, 90–92
    trying new, 13–14

Ford, Harrison, 44

G
Gandhi, Mahatma, 61
Garnett, Laura, 27–28
Gifford, Kathie Lee, 42
goals
    as dream with deadline, 97–98, 99
    establishment of, 100–102
    list of goals/actions, 92–94
    for Renewal Plan, 96–97
    selection of one goal, 94–95
gossip chain, 14
Gross, Michael, 39
growth
    as reason for renewal, 80–81
    in SIGNs, 29, 30
    time for renewal, knowledge of, 47

H
Hakala-Ausperk, Catherine, 64
Hamm, Trent, 59, 65–66
happiness
    mission and, 19
    values/accomplishment matching
      and, 12–13
health
    as reason to quit job, 79–80
    work/life balance and, 62–64
How Do You Do It?
    action, measurement of, 98–99
    action, preparation for, 90–92
    do something about your job,
      88–90
    first step, taking, 87
    goal as dream with deadline, 97–98
    goals, picking one, 94–95
    goals/actions, list of, 92–94
    goals/objectives, establishment of,
      100–102
    plan, final sections of, 92
    Renewal Plan, actions for goals,
      102–104

Renewal Plan, completion of,
    104–105
Renewal Plan, how answer, 96–97
Renewal Plan, time commitment, 100
situations to avoid, 95–96

I
IBM, 53
identity
    list of what you did, 22–24
    respect for true identity, 96
    true, 22
    See also Who Are You?
imperfection, 96
improvement, process of, 96
instinct, 28, 29

J
job
    doing something about, 88–90
    list of what you did, 22–24
    list of what you do now, 24–25
    protection of, 75
    security, 60
    signs of hating job, 78–79
job, staying or leaving
    consideration of, 88–90
    decision about, 51–52
    in-between jobs stage, 65–66
    quitting job, final steps before, 64–65
    reasons for, 52–64
    selection of next job, 66
    See also Where Should You Be?
Jobs, Steve, 82, 83–84
Johnson, Shana Montesol, 5
joy, 20

K
King, Stephen, 44

L
learning
    continuous, 14

professional development
    continuing with, 14
    as key to success, 81
    responsibility for your own growth,
        56–57
    See also learning
professional influence, 94
purpose
    creation of, 58
    identification of your story and, xviii
    life cycle of, 46–47
    moving closer to, 37
    as reason for renewal, 80

R
Rath, Tom, 76
relationship
    with boss, 54–55
    change of relationships at work, 82
    with colleagues, 61
    improvement goal, 93
renewal
    benefits of moving forward, 71–72
    definition of, 2
    5W1H for Renewal Plan, xvii–xx
    in-between jobs stage, 65–66
    by making a difference, xix
    plateauing as sign of need for,
        44–45
    reasons for, 77–84
    rejuvenation in any situation with,
        15–16
    Roz Savage on, 3
    selection of next job, 66
    values, consideration about, 4–7
    where it should take place, 51–52
    why your career/life are worth
        renewing, 17
    worries about change, 72–77
Renewal Plan
    actions for goals, 102–104
    completion of, 104–105
    copy of, 107–109

development of personal, xiv
    5W1H for, xvii–xx
    goal, selection of one, 94–95
    how answer, 96–97
    step one, 7–8
    time commitment, 100
    time decision, 48
    values, personal, 7–8
    what you want to do, 31–32
    where decision, 67
    why statement, 84–85
    writing in, 101–102
respect
    attitude in workplace and, 64
    between boss/employee, 55
resume, 14
retirement, 45–46
RIFFED (reduction in force), 60
risk
    fear of, 74
    safety nets for, 75–77
Roosevelt, Franklin, 77
Rubin, Gretchen, 13

S
safety net
    family/friends, 75–76
    protection of job, 75
    sanity, preservation of, 76–77
salary, 54
    See also money
Savage, Roz, 3, 7
scheduling, 98–99
security, 60
self-improvement, 93
Sheperd, Scott, 16
SIGNs, 28–30
"The Simple Dollar" website, 59
skills, 81
sleep, 62
so what question, 4
staff, 61
starting over, 64